hand wash cold

care instructions
for an ordinary life

KAREN MAEZEN MILLER

MJF BOOKS
New York

Published by MJF Books
Fine Communications
322 Eighth Avenue
New York, NY 10001

Hand Wash Cold
LC Control Number: 2011938938
ISBN-13: 978-1-60671-116-3
ISBN-10: 1-60671-116-4

QF   10   9   8   7   6   5   4   3   2   1

Dedicated to all my female ancestors
whose names have been lost or forgotten,
and especially to my grandmothers,
Erma Cordelia Null
and Hedwig Alvina Winkler,
who wrung everything out and hung it on a line

What is the Way?
Ordinary mind is the Way.

— ANCIENT ZEN LAUNDRY INSTRUCTIONS

contents

PART THREE

the yard: *To Forget Oneself Is
to Be Enlightened by the Ten Thousand Things*

prologue

Care Instructions

S OME MONTHS AGO I ordered a suit of monk's clothing from Japan. It was a set of *samue* ('sa-mu-ay). Samue is streetwear for Zen monks and priests, a simple wide-sleeved wraparound jacket with matching pull-on pants. It's an everyday outfit that's easy to throw on when you're not traipsing around in your robes. But the truth is, I don't often traipse around in my robes. I'm not really that kind of Zen priest, not the kind you have pictured in your mind. Even though I ordered them all the way from Japan, I've never worn my special pants or jacket. I just wear the same kinds of clothes you do, while doing the same kinds of things you do, every day.

What was more useful to me than the clothing was a tiny piece of paper that came tucked inside my shipment: a three-inch square of deckle-edged rice paper printed in Japanese. Because I had no idea what it said, I found it charming. I imagined it might be laundry instructions such as "Hand wash cold." Or perhaps it said "Inspected by No. 12." I put it on my desk, where I still look at it all the time.

Later I learned that the tag described the fabric's natural chestnut dye, but the translation didn't matter. My delight in the indecipherable had shown me something profound. With only a change in one's perspective, the most ordinary things take on inexpressible beauty. When we don't know, we don't judge. And when we don't judge, we see things in a different light.

That's why I wrote this book. To atone for the messes I've made, to see the wisdom I've overlooked, to offer the care I've left undone, to show both you and me the inexpressible beauty that comes tucked inside an ordinary life.

Dogen Zenji, a thirteenth-century Japanese Zen Buddhist monk, once summarized the spiritual path in three lines:

> To study the Way is to study oneself.
> To study oneself is to forget oneself.
> To forget oneself is to be enlightened by the ten
> thousand things.

He wasn't speaking only about his life or my life, or only about the Buddhist path or any other devoutly religious pursuit. He was talking about you, and in between the lines of this book, so am I.

This book has three parts. The first part is about doing the laundry, revealing the pure wisdom that resides within you. The second part is about washing the dishes, bringing that wisdom to life as compassionate action. The third part is about tending the yard, sowing peace in the patch of pavement and grass you inhabit.

This sequence is not my idea, although it has been my experience. It is the teaching of the masters and the way of ordinary life. See for yourself.

PART ONE

the laundry

To Study the Way
Is to Study Oneself

$\backsim$

Full Basket

a life as told by laundry

by SEPTEMBER EVERYTHING WAS GONE. Given away or sold cheap. Every stick of the living room furniture went to my sister, who hired movers to take it. Two garage sales emptied the shelves. The full set of crystal from my wedding registry, still in plastic in the original shipping box, sold for thirty-five dollars. The buyer halfheartedly bargained — "Is this set complete?" — before she laughed at her own question and handed over the bills. One Sunday night I invited the little guy from the aerobics class inside and sold him the wine rack for twenty dollars. He'd wanted dinner and a date, but he drove away with the rack standing up in the backseat of his MG convertible.

I kept what I needed and wanted. They'd become the same. The bed, desk, books, a chair, and about half my clothes. I sublet one room, the smaller one, in a two-bedroom apartment from someone who seemed desperate for the company and the cash. I did what everyone else had already done at the big house on Avalon Drive: I left. And then, after two years in a falling market, the house finally sold. The closing date drew near.

It was time to take care of the last bit of housekeeping. Just a day's worth, a day in September.

There was stuff left in drawers and closets, like the cabinets above and below the tiny wet bar between the kitchen and the living room with the blue-and-yellow-tile counter. An understated spot that had made the house seem so authentic. *This would make someone a lovely home*, I often thought, realizing it wasn't me. I surveyed the mismatched glassware and souvenir mugs, the army of half-empty liquor bottles my husband had brought home after doing beverage inventory at the hotel he managed. We can't use it there, he'd said. We never used it here, either. I poured every bottle down the little sink and stuck the empties, like bones, into garbage bags. Dragged outside, the bags piled up behind the little white picket sanitation fence by the garage. Up and over the top, an embarrassing tower of unmade toasts.

Upstairs, I swept through the closets of empty hangers and leftover shoes, pausing over a stash of get-well cards from my surgery five years earlier, when the doctor said, "Get pregnant now," and, looking at my blank-faced husband, I knew I didn't love him.

I pulled down the attic stairs and went up. In some ways, it was my favorite room. We'd bought the house from a surgeon, and that explained the precision of the place. No visible scars. The guy had actually done his own gardening and cleaned his own pool, installed his own sprinkler system and outdoor lights. Awash in aftershave, I imagined, with an aperitif in hand.

The attic was high-ceilinged and light. The span was clean and shadowless. The surgeon had put in a solid floor and neatly lain old doors and shutters across the rafters in case someone could use them again. On one wall was a built-in shelf where I kept my small store of Christmas decorations. There weren't enough ornaments to cover a tree, but there were centerpieces and ceramics I'd set out in the years before I could no longer lift the sentiment.

I saw an unfamiliar bag and opened it. Inside was a jumble of clothes like a forgotten load of laundry. I couldn't remember the clothes, but tipped my head in and recognized the scent. It was the smell of excitement and fearlessness, of love and optimism, all run out. It was my someday, my glorious one day, the one that had never arrived. And here I sat, snorting a sudden gust of wistfulness from a sack of dirty socks and shirts.

Life is laundry.

When I say that, I don't mean I do *a lot* of laundry, although I do. I just started my fifth load this week and it's only Tuesday. Still, some folks do more and some folks do less. Either way, that's not the point.

I don't mean my life is *like* laundry, although it is. Troubles pile up, and I ignore them as long as I can. Just about the time I sort through the heap, clean it, and stash it away, it reappears and I have to take care of it all over again. So yes, life is like laundry, but that's not what I mean, either.

I mean life *is* laundry, and when you do not yet see that your life is laundry, you may not see your life clearly at all. You might think, for instance, that the life you have is not at all the life you had in mind and so it doesn't constitute your real life at all. Your real life is the life you pine for, the life you're planning or the life you've already lost, the life fulfilled by the person, place, and sexy new front-loading washer of your dreams. This is the life we are most devoted to: the life we don't have.

When I was thirty-five, I looked up one day and realized that I hadn't had a life. Oh, I'd had a lot of things. I'd had a husband and a marriage of sorts. In fact, I still did. Between us, we had two late-model cars, two high-speed careers, and a two-story house on an oak-lined street where people left their blinds open so everyone else could look in and sigh. I had a great job working with talented and energetic people at my own company. I worked too hard, but I made enough money. I had a pool and even a little pool house, neither of which I ever found the time or friends to fill. I had my youth. I had my looks, and I had the self-devotion to maintain them at any cost. I had fancy jewelry and cookware for which I had no use. What I did not have was laundry.

I had no laundry. I had clothing, and plenty of it, but I also had Theresa, who week after week did lifetimes' worth of other

6

people's laundry, including my own. For more than ten years running, Theresa came to my house each Wednesday when no one
was home. Except for the rare coincidence when I might be way-
laid in bed by the sniffles, I never saw her come, I never saw her
leave, and I never saw what she did in between. In this way, we
had the strangest kind of intimacy.

She saw my underwear. She soaked my stains. She smelled my
sweat. She did the same for my husband, all of which I refused to
do. She swept and polished, emptied the trash and the hampers,
and filled the house with a heady haze of lemony pine. Upstairs,
on opposite sides of our bed, she laid our warm, clean laundry
folded in his and her stacks. Everything was in its place. Only it
wasn't my place, because it wasn't my life. My life was going to
begin on some other day, when I had myself situated in some
better place.

All those years she laundered my hidden self, I never knew
much about Theresa. Because I lived in southeast Texas at the
time, it wasn't so unusual that she was Creole, her people from
Louisiana. She had a lilt in her voice, a kind of saucy French accent thrice removed, and her stories were spicy and colorful. She
had truckloads of men and kids, problems everywhere, things to
fix for five hundred miles in all directions. We'd learn about these
in notes she left behind, or in calls to reschedule in calamity's
wake. She had a real life, it seemed, and I didn't.

Just as I never touched a stitch of dirty laundry, I stood at
an antiseptic distance from everything in my life. And who
wouldn't? To my critical eye, everything around me needed so

much improvement. My relationship with my husband needed fix-ing, but that was largely up to him. He had a lot of changing to do. My work was a problem, what with the long hours and troublesome employees. Good people were hard to find. My friendships were scant because I didn't have the time or an interest in people who weren't like me. I had so little in common with ordinary women.

As you might expect of someone with such unrelenting stan-dards, much of what was simple about life was beneath me. Not quite beneath, but certainly too trivial to mess with. I bought into the view that life was a transaction, and that time was money. Since I had proven I could make a respectable living using my time in one way, I outsourced just about every other thing there was to do. I had a cleaning lady and a pool man. I had a yardman and an old guy who came around every spring and cleaned my rain gutters. We ate out. Our cars were hand washed and polished by someone else. My secretary addressed my Christmas cards. I had a manicurist and a hair stylist and, even more, a hair colorist, none of whom I could live more than one month without. My closest relationships were with the retainers and surrogates who tended my self-image.

There is nothing inherently wrong with any of this; these are choices many people make, and I still make some of them. What was wrong was that I was numbingly unfulfilled. I was deeply angry and silently, sleeplessly anxious. I thought I was working harder than anyone, and yet I was missing what everyone else seemed so easily to grasp. A life.

And I *was* missing it, because I thought life was something other than my life. I thought life was something envisioned and achieved. I thought it was manufactured from ideals and earned through elbow grease. I thought it was yet to arrive, and so I missed everything that had already come. I was blind to my marriage and my absence from it. I saw my job almost exclusively as a necessity and rarely as the exhilarating invention that it was. My home was a headache, a pile of rust and dust. I was certain that I never wanted a family: not one more person to clean up after. And I had never examined my mind, my heart, or my hand in any of this.

When I finally did lift a finger, it was just to nudge this lifeless, loveless world asunder.

"Why don't you leave?" I asked my husband one day after work. It was not an unusual day. Nothing had been said. Nothing had happened. It was a day like any other that I'd hauled across the wide river of my discontent.

He left.

It wasn't quite the end, but it was the beginning of the end of something that was already over. After a few squalls about money and other things that stand for money — rights, obligations, fairness, and furniture — the divorce was done. But the undoing wasn't.

A few months after my husband left, I started to worry that the problem might not have been my husband.

I took a lover and fell quickly overboard. After that lover left, and the lover after that, I started to worry that the problem might not have been the lover.

I sold my business. After the business sold, I started to worry that the problem might not have been the business.

I left the house, and after I left, I started to worry that the problem might not have been the house.

In the attic that last day, kneeling over a bag of stale and wrinkled recollections, I had a hint of what I had been missing. Laundry. And not just laundry, but what laundry gives us: an honest encounter with ourselves before we're freshened and fluffed and sanitized. Before we have ourselves put together again.

Do your own laundry, and the tag inside will tell you exactly how to care for what you hold in your hands. Every bit of life comes with instructions when we are attentive enough to notice, and on the high bluff of my prime I hadn't yet opened my eyes.

I gave that sack of old clothes away, but soon, and every day after, I took back a bit more of the load I had long foisted on someone else. I took back responsibility for myself, my relationships, my work, my days, my nights, my joy, my love, my pain, my happiness. I took on the washing, drying, and folding that constitute an authentic life.

I began to excavate what all the ancients, and my own spiritual forebears, tell us we can find at the very bottom of the basket, beneath our rumpled, stained, and worn-out lives. I went looking for a change of clothes, and I found the path to clear wisdom, compassion, and enlightenment. Bit by bit, I reassembled the remnants of my discarded life and made myself happy and whole. I can tell you how. It begins with the laundry, and it leads everywhere you never thought you'd go.

❧

CHAPTER 2

Handle with Care
some shrinkage will occur

I T HAD ONCE SEEMED EXOTIC, like the smell of places I'd never been, a secret world, an extravagant dream. Now there was one name for the aroma in the attic, and it wasn't Husband. It was Him.

Our happenstance meeting in a restaurant down the street three months after my marriage quietly ended. My heart-pounding drive home. The still, sure hush before the phone rang the first time, him at home a thousand miles away, me on my back in the dark. Four days later, my last-minute, first-class flight up to sleep with a stranger. The hotel room where he knocked, carrying wild-flowers, and where I studied his unrecognizable face. The music, the meals, the endearments, the habit he made of calling me Sweet. Thanksgiving in Santa Fe in the snow and the firelight, every shimmer sanctified by the arrogant absolution of our one true love. All the beds and showers and airports and love made coming and going. And the hand-penned story that arrived in a box for my birthday, the story that ended "and the universe became their own." His urgent drive down in the old Audi to stay, with hallowed books and hiking boots and a duffel of romantic destiny, when the bag of attic-bound clothes had arrived. The terrible year when everything turned and dropped and terrified me, sleep snuck out like tide, and I finally stood hysterical, sobbing, stiff against the sound of his sure-footed leaving. Every late-night ramble through every room in my house and my head, every wail and every gasp and every shameful time I punched in the long-distance number, no way to brace against the certain fall. Days and weeks and months, nearly a year until the phone rang on its own. He hadn't called for any reason, he said. Perhaps it was to hear me ask the question that I couldn't stop from asking. "Yes, as a matter of fact, I am in love with her," he said.

Downstairs, a friend was calling my name. The cheery, faithful one who had promised to drop by to help me finish the house by late afternoon. We met on the attic stairs, where she took the bag from me and glanced inside.

"Salvation Army?"

All that, in one whiff.

I'd started in on this story earlier but got lost in the telling, as can happen when we make things up. We make a story of our lives, and we don't much care for a simple one. So we embroider with feathers and lace and antique buttons pilfered from grandma's chifforobe. Or we rip out the seams, lengthen the hem, and sew something else more to our liking. We do this all the time, with nearly every sigh and backward glance, and so we hardly ever see what is really in our hands.

In my case, a bag of old stuff. Just a bag of old stuff.

Everything else I'd crammed into the attic stash was my invention, a sickening bouquet of memory, ache, and martyrdom, but I called it my truth. For sure, I once thought this sack of crap was the truest thing I'd ever known.

You might have a bag like this in your own attic. You might call it Her, or Then, or When, or If Only.

The short of it was, I'd fallen in love. I'd fallen in love not with my husband, whose uneventful company I'd kept for a decade, but with a mysterious drifter. That much was fact, but I'd adorned it, in the falling, with layers of meaning and promise. I'd explored it first with desperate lust and longing, then plumbed it with poetic grievance. My love for the fellow had hardly lasted a year, but my love for the loss loomed eternal. That's what I'd found in the bag — that's what we all find whenever we go looking in all-too-familiar places: pain.

This book is a love story. Every life is a love story, but few of us know what love is until the story is nearly over.

We spend most of our lives thinking love is a feeling. Sometimes we even feel it. We look for it, we wish for it, we revel in it, we grab and clutch, only to lose it, then travel the world to find it again. But love is not a feeling. And that particular feeling we call love never lasts. Everything — every feeling, every face, every filament — shrinks and fades and falls apart. Nothing stays brand-new. What becomes of a life fashioned of such flimsy fiber?

I can't recall the first time I fell in love. Certainly I felt the hot flush of teenage need, the reckless rush to lose my lonely goodness. A schoolgirl, I cruised the hot nights of north Texas under the influence of bad boys and strawberry wine. I worshipped the unattainable and settled for whoever knocked on the door. Mine was the adolescent's double life of close calls and intact curfews. But my recollections are certainly wrong — all recollections are — enlivened today by the seasoning of fresh sentiment and memory's selective service.

I know I didn't feel like a teenager when I married my first husband, and by that standard, I suppose I didn't love him. Love simply never entered the picture. *I married him because he asked me*, I used to say with a shrug, and for the longest time I thought that ugly honesty surely indicted me as a fool. On the contrary, given the limitations of reason, it was the best reason of all.

Just twenty-three years old, I had a college degree, my first job, and no conflicting direction or distraction. The man who asked for my hand was older, taller, stronger, could slam a long ball over the left-center fence, and possessed a qualification that I found compelling at the time: he owned a full set of dinnerware.

This sounds like a joke, but it is both accurate and meaningful. We seek in our lovers and mates the illusion of completion, a handheld wholeness that is life's eternal mission. It's just not a mission that we can accomplish, very often, as missionaries.

My betrothed had plates. He had furniture. He had a perfectly fine job and a perfectly fine place, and I could imagine myself being perfectly fine in it. Imagination is integral to this kind of endeavor, this kind of fantasy. When imagination took hold, it moved right in and made this chapter of my life legal and binding.

It is revealing to me now that, back then, I didn't want to make a fuss about this marriage. I didn't want to have a wedding. I didn't want to spend the money. I didn't want to buy a dress or take the time. I didn't want to bear his name or wear a ring, and I didn't want to have his children. In my own defense, I concluded that I was being modern. I meant no harm. Nothing about it had much meaning at all, certainly not the archaic vows I spoke in a half-price hotel suite before immediate family only. I agreed to it because I was ready to grow up and get on with things. It seemed like the time to do the next thing, and the next thing was, he asked.

This is how wisdom subtly guides us in the direction we'd least like to go.

Too quickly I found out that there was little about this husband of mine that I actually cared for. We conventionally call this part of marriage *after the honeymoon*, and it begins, shockingly enough, immediately after the honeymoon. It turned out I didn't really like his last name, for instance, and so I didn't use it. I didn't like his hair and could foresee how soon there would be even less of it to dislike, the disappearance of which I *really* didn't like. I didn't like the shape of his nose. I didn't like much of what he said, or even the words he sometimes misused in speaking, and the unpolished roughness of his Rust Belt vernacular. All of it wore on me, and since there wasn't much depth of devotion in me to wear out, I was done in no time.

You could probably say much the same for other marriages, because marriage seems to give us far more of what we dislike in one another than what we like. We might quickly conclude that we chose poorly: erring by type, looks, interests, values, background, or beliefs. This may be the case, but it's still irrelevant. It's what we do with our mismatch that matters. Deep, transformational love is born out of what you don't much like at all.

Life did have that kind of transcendent love in store for me — it stands in perpetual reserve and reward for us all — on the day I stopped looking for something else.

That day, I'm sorry to say, was a long way away.

When everything had stopped between my husband and me except time's passage, I consoled myself with easy explanations: *We are married to our jobs.* With convenient blame: *He's never really loved me.* And with corrosive judgment: *I deserve better.* I had matured from a naive know-nothing into a woman with ideals. Ideals can be a disruptive thing.

I now had a much clearer notion of what an ideal marriage should be and had no doubt it wasn't the one I had. Nearly all of us amass a set of ideals as we advance in life — ideal love; ideal marriage; ideal job; ideal home; ideal looks, hair, skin, and weight; the ideal strategy to convey us safely to an ideal future. All of these will be reliably stripped from our grip in time, but not until we spend most of our lives fine-tuning our standards, trading one failed ideal for a more promising one.

There is always a more promising ideal. When it appears as a breaking light above the dark horizon, a halo cresting above a colorless cloudbank of boredom, it can look really promising.

It *was*. It was the promise of my personal life catastrophe, arriving right on schedule.

Soon after my husband backed out of the driveway, I met a handsome stranger, handed him my every desire, and in the time it took to enrobe myself in a new and improved fantasy, got dumped. By the natural law governing insane attractions, he seemed to be everything I wasn't. He was tall, daring, opinionated, overeducated, unemployed, and a Zen Buddhist, for Christ's sake. Other than that, our pairing was completely unoriginal. It was the *real thing*, we proved to one another in outrageous displays of devotion, about six months before it became a very *unreal thing*.

There's not much more I need to say about a hard fall and a broken heart. Everyone knows all there is to know about it, since it happens a million times a minute. It's what we do with our disappointment that makes a difference.

We talk about it, of course, over and over. We talk until our family is first worried sick about us and then just sick of us. We talk until friends stop calling back or recognizing us in the grocery store. We talk to therapists, so many therapists and drug dispensers, who may not be too terribly inclined to help us change the subject. We write about it, we read about it, we sing about it, and we cry. Lordy, we cry.

The most I ever cried in public was in a movie theater watching Meg Ryan swoon for Tom Hanks in the romantic comedy *Sleepless in Seattle*. It wasn't the story that got to me, although the subject of soul mates is not a safe topic for consideration so soon after fate has ditched you on the muddy shoulder of the road. I started bawling from the first croaking note of "As Time Goes By" sung by Jimmy Durante over the opening credits. I didn't stop for 105 minutes.

> It's still the same old story
> A fight for love and glory
> A case of do or die.
> The world will always welcome lovers
> As time goes by.

Sniff. The year of my grieving I must have lost two full sizes in saltwater weight.

It's not so easy to be done with your own sob story. We might set it down for a time, but we hardly ever get rid of it. Provoked, we haul out the old emotional wardrobe and put it on again. We're so accustomed to familiar, wounded feelings and self-serving narratives — they caress us like the gentle fold of an old T-shirt, the nub of a well-worn weave — that we mistakenly think they're who we are. We think we are our thoughts; we think we are our feelings; we think we are nothing more than a bulging basket of past experiences.

Can we really find happiness by letting go of what we know of ourselves? It is the only way.

Shortly after I'd written my recollections from moving day, five years after the events had occurred and twelve years before today, I handed the pristine pages to my mother to read. It was one of the first things I'd written in my own voice, from my own life, and I wanted my mother to see me, finally, for the person I thought I was. I handed it to her tentatively, as though I might startle her with my indiscretion. She read it and scooted it back to me over the smooth surface of my kitchen table. "Very emotional," she said, and nothing more.

Now a mother, I hear her terse words so lovingly. She knew far better than me who I was and who I wasn't. She didn't mistake me for my feelings any more than I would mistake my two-year-old for her tantrums, or my ten-year-old for her anguished tearburst. I was so much more than my emotions; we are all so much more than our emotions; but I couldn't yet sort that out for myself.

Like clothes left too long in a hamper, my story was still on the stinky side.

I've since had more practice separating the lights from the darks, the shrinkable cottons from the indestructible polyester, the cause from the effect, and the present from the past. I've had more practice washing and wringing and handling with care. So you'll understand why I must now apologize to all the innocent men I harmed by my wretched carelessness, on whom I placed the burden of my yearning and the blame for my despair. In matters of the heart, we too often forget what we have promised to remember, and remember what is best to forget.

"Salvation Army?" my friend had asked.

Yes.

She was the scout for the rescue mission, the first of a noble brigade. The one being saved was me.

CHAPTER 3

Lights and Darks

no whiter whites or brighter colors

O
H, HOW I NEEDED SAVING. I was a refugee from my own life. I was the captive of what might have been. I was depressed. Big time.

In that effortless way available to those dining on three square meals of dejection, I had stopped eating.

In the way slumber escapes when every waking hour is drugged by pitch-black dreams, I had stopped sleeping.

I had stopped seeing, hearing, and noticing anything but my own sadness. I had stopped thinking it had ever been otherwise, and stopped believing it would ever end. I had come to the curve in the road that we mistake for a destination, a conclusion that convinces us, for a wallowing width of time, that we've come far enough. I had arrived at a diagnosis. It was mostly a self-diagnosis, and so it fit me like my own skin.

I was a victim. Yes, that's what I was. Of bad choices and of bad people. Of hard luck and of worse timing. Of every wrong turn and missed signal and circumstances beyond my control. The sadness was certain now, certifiable, chronic, and biochemical. Furthermore, it was not my fault.

One day after a deadening nine hours of pretending to work, I drove up the drive and into my emptied garage. I reached above me to where the garage door opener was clipped to the driver's-side visor. I pushed the button and watched the door descend in the reflection in my rearview mirror. I did this without turning off the car's engine. I sat in the airless dark and let the motor whine. Not for long, but for long enough.

In an instant, I pushed the door lift again, and let the light rise. Turning off the key, I opened the car door and stepped out.

Just like that, I stepped out.

Later, I could have said this was the moment I saved my own life. At the time, it felt more like I'd outed myself from a high-stakes game of masquerade. I didn't want to die. I didn't want to play sad anymore. I wanted to live live live live live. Who was I fooling?

The answer was, I was no longer fooling myself.

Something had shifted in that garage. Something had switched while I idled in the cool leather contours of my black BMW. I had shifted from *reverse*, from a backward and distorted obsession with my life as it wasn't, into another gear. It wasn't yet *drive*, that take-charge throttle toward a *better* future, an illusory aim that can send you careening just as blindly. No, my new speed was no speed. I was in neutral. Having driven myself to the brink of noxious extinction, I simply decided to coast.

Coasting is a largely underrated mode of transport. Yet it is fairly certain to require the least effort and, consequently, to effect the least harm. We should all take our foot off the pedal more often and see where the downhill glide takes us. We might be surprised at the view.

No longer trusting my solitary amusements, I sought company. Not company, mind you, with which to *talk about* my problems, but to not talk about my problems, and this is a critical difference. In the parlance of a spiritual process, this stage of self-awareness is sometimes called "getting sick of your sickness." It's the one sickness that cures all ills.

I dropped in at the gym where I had lately poured myself into a near-religious pursuit of skeletal perfection. My trainer looked at me with alarm. He pointed at the door I'd just come in and ordered me back out again.

"You look like you need a cheeseburger," he said.

I went straight to the fast-food place next door and downed a double patty. All 540 calories shot straight into my veins like liquid sunshine.

I called a buddy, a middle-aged divorced man who had recently come out to a circle of friends as gay. He'd been the one to take all my tear-soaked 2 AM telephone calls, lulling my fitful rage and cushioning my dying hopes in the gentle darkness before so many dawns. I suspect his own experience had sharpened his sensors for camouflage. He cut through civilities. "Come over here right now," he told me.

I went over without stopping, since I'd become an instantaneous convert to the faultless wisdom of following instructions.

His apartment was the kind I'd passed through immediately after college, a temporary spot on my way up and out to a life of grander dimension. It was a squat, square box in one of the zillion cookie-cutter complexes that littered the fast-growing suburban fringe of the city. Like those of us gathered there on this day, the flat had seen better days. The dingy white walls were scuffed and gouged; the carpet was worn; the gold-flecked Formica and metallic wallpaper recalled a decade better left behind.

It was a sight for sore eyes, a refuge outside my own head. This place with someone to talk to other than *me*, surrounded by things other than *mine*, with occupations other than *myself*, would become my safe harbor for the next year.

He seemed to know I needed the comfort of having nothing to do. He worked from home, and so I listened to him talk on the phone, calmed by the cackle of a conversation I didn't understand. He moved about doing unremarkable things — typing on a keyboard, tossing paper into the trash, going to the bathroom — and I was serenely transfixed by a scene free of my own tiresome commentary. Leaning against a dusty bookshelf, I saw a title that thwacked me from my trancelike state into full attention.

KAREN, the spine read, THIS IS ABOUT YOU.

The book was actually titled *Control Theory: A New Explanation of How We Control Our Lives*. It was the last book I would have ever chosen to put in front of me, in part because I hadn't yet read what the author, William Glasser, MD, would shout to me on its pages, about how the actions and thoughts we choose directly control our present life, and that all of us everywhere live miserable lives of our own miserable *choosing*, until we *choose* otherwise. A few years later the work would be renamed *Choice Theory*. Good choice.

On this night I was marooned with no choice, void of preference or aversion, and I picked the book up and took it into the spare bedroom with me. I did not sleep until I'd read every page of it, and when I did close my eyes it was to full, surrendered slumber. In the morning, I called my doctor, the one whom I'd coaxed into prescribing an antidepressant with which I clearly couldn't cope, and I said, "I'm going to do this on my own."

I'd woken up to the task of taking care of myself.

And here I clarify that it is not my intention with this testimonial to make light of depression or any kind of suffering. I intend only to point out the greater mass of it that is self-inflicted as a result of our habits of mind. These days it is hard for me to find any suffering that I do not inflict on myself, over and over, any problem that isn't born of my own fear and brittle judgment, again and again, any impossibility that doesn't arise from my own parsimonious view: the view that what I am and what I have is not enough. Never enough.

Insufficiency can be our most cherished possession. We wear it like a permanent stain. That's why everything they keep selling us, and everything we keep buying, is some kind of soap.

Worn out and fading fast? You need triple-strength color guard.

Damaged goods? You need dual-action dirt fighters.

Unlovable? You need nature's secret springtime fragrance boosters.

Not true, except by believing, we make it so.

This is the little-known secret to a life of happy laundering: there are no whiter whites or brighter colors, no matter what kind of soap you're swallowing. What's more, when we release ourselves from judgment and inadequacy, we free everyone else from our criticism and blame.

No, it is not my intention to make light of depression, but with millions and ever more millions suffering in unremitting darkness, abetted and affirmed by chronic diagnoses and chronic treatments, isn't it time someone made light of it? Could there be another way to approach life besides grim endurance and abject helplessness?

How do we go deeper than the deepest reach of our own sullied self-narrative? I was about to find out.

A new path had appeared by morning. I was still wishing for what I wanted, but miraculously, finding what I needed on a breadcrumb trail leading to a home I never knew I'd left.

◡

CHAPTER 4

Toughest Stains

getting out the traces of self

h OME WAS A FUNNY WORD TO ME THEN, since I couldn't remember living anywhere that came close.

I'd been born in California, the second child of a sturdy college girl from Texas and a hard-luck West Coast hot-rodder. Lucky for me, I was the granddaughter of a big-shouldered Illinois Irishman who'd come west to the golden brink for a better life. All told, we were three little granddaughters, each loved so strongly that none doubted she was Grandpa's favorite or that his house was where we belonged.

At home with Mom and Dad was a prickly place where the air sometimes froze and the ground swayed and the safest place to be was tucked out of sight. You could find me there, or you might not look.

Grandpa's was different. It was a little patch of parched ground at the end of the road called the Road to Grandpa's, an hour or so up the way from our starter house in LA, and reached long after the littlest one in the backseat asked, "Are we still in California?" His was a tidy four-room box of a handmade house in an orange grove ocean with a mountain in the distance, a mountain with a name we all knew because Grandpa always called it by name, Torrey Mountain, the way he called everything by name — by the names he gave, if there were none, to pet pigeons and doves and chickens, and to the rooster and duck and dogs, and sometimes to cats, my grandmother, my sisters, and me, the one he called My Little Irisher.

We would tumble out of the station wagon on these trips, which must have been weekly when we were young, and my parents were achingly young, and the cord that connected us all was noose tight and not yet torn. We rambled into the dusty earth and through the endless rows of citrus trees that stretched on forever, at least until the highway, where Grandpa's two-acre spread played out.

First, yes, there were the oranges, special oranges that would be the very Sunkist oranges you saw advertised on TV, that had to be irrigated on rare and significant days known as Irrigation Days, which were serious from beginning to end and produced the most luscious grade of mud. We were allowed to squish through it calf-high in the game known as Grand Central Station, we little girls having no idea what a grand or a central or a station might otherwise be. Then there were the rose bushes, giant, with blooms that dwarfed my head when Grandma propped me there to pose for the photo album. There was the honeysuckle vine that crept up over the shade arbor, whose blossoms had the tiniest little string that you pulled so carefully and touched to your tongue, *Yes, yes, I can taste it!* There were the tree swings and the black barrel barbecue for marshmallows, and the push-up popsicles kept in the forbidden freezer drawer.

There were so many long, sunshiny days with water-sprinkler chases and front-room dance recitals, sing-alongs to Patsy Cline, and pitted olives in a glass dish on the dinner table. I always popped the olives like palace guard hats on my fingertips and ate them one by one, and Grandpa laughed every time as if he'd never seen anything like it.

Those might be any of the days, but every night ended in the same way, in the ritual scent of Old Spice aftershave. Grandpa shaved in the evenings because he got up before dawn. Oranges were a life but they weren't a living. He worked for the oil company on Torrey Mountain, wearing blue work pants and carrying a painted black lunch box, and when he got up in the dark to get ready, I got up with him. He would fix a mug of coffee for himself and one for me too in a tiny Tupperware cup, mostly milk and two sugar cubes, and we would face the day in a fearless way, sitting in silence side by side.

And if it could ever be so, this was a place where leaving, even the leaving, was the best part. Grandpa would load us in his car for the two-minute drive into town, park along the crumbling curb and open the screen door to Lechler's Grocery. *These are my grandbabies, Harry*, he'd announce as we three little ones shyly advanced on the cool cement floor. Harry would then fix up three identical bags of penny candy for the trip home. When the dentist decreed and Mom imposed an end to this, Grandpa replaced the candy with two dollars each and took us to Lechler's just for the showing off.

Later, when I wasn't nearly as small or cute anymore, but Grandpa still glowed at the sight of me, we moved to Texas. Dad had moved out first and alone, starting a job and finding a brand-new house with a matchbox bedroom for each of us. My big sister graduated from eighth grade, and we loaded up the new Ford Torino station wagon, my mom and we girls. We drove off and left California, the oranges, and Grandpa and Grandma. Somewhere on the highway in Arizona or New Mexico, we heard a thudding crash and pulled over to see Mom's master's degree typewriter, a hallowed thing, a centerpiece of our lives and a fixture on the dining room table for as long as we could remember, smashed in a heap of smithereens in the middle of the road. It had flown off the wagon roof.

Things weren't tied down so well after all.

Mom stood helplessly on the roadside in the desert wind. Watching from the backseat, I stifled tears for her, the tears I would weep in my princess canopy bed during the late-night shouts in the living room in the years to come.

Home became a distant thing. I would write "Santa Monica"

in the blank beside "Birthplace," all those vowels imparting a far-away status. But we hardly ever returned there, until we never went back at all. My grandparents became faint and frail, even by phone. Grandma died first, a long and bitter retreat. Then Grandpa came to Texas for his turn. He was stooped and stale and forgetful, forgetting even to buckle his belt, since he couldn't unbuckle it again. I had learned more about him by then: who he wasn't. He wasn't big and never had been, being a half-foot short of six feet tall. By then a young woman, I'd already begun to choose big boys and men to stand beside, only later realizing the misperception. To a four-year-old, five foot six was big enough.

I held fast to what I'd later learned, the family scandals and perpetual failings, and forgot the rest. I forgot about California. Only recently, in the long sad summer that had just ended, and at the suggestion of a counselor running low on weekly advice, had I looked through Grandma's photo albums, now in my closet, with open eyes. I saw myself again, and I was stunned.

I was a happy girl.

There, I said it. Happy.

By this time I had a laundry list of labels for myself, and Happy wasn't one of them. I was the Quiet One, for instance. A Middle Child. A High Achiever, and a People Pleaser. A Good Speller. A Worrywart. A Cynic. A Morning Person. Perfectionist. Top of My Class. Type A. Workaholic. Passive-Aggressive. Relationship-Phobic.

Control Freak. Adult Child of Alcoholic with Abandonment Issues. A Transient Insomniac and Borderline Exercise Addict.

Okay, I'm making some of this up, but I'm not making all of it up. I'd paid good money for help assembling this Frankenstein of a self-image. No wonder I was hurting all over.

The way we seem to do things, in this world that prizes critical thinking as its highest output, is to put a label on everything. If we name it — the thinking goes — we can know it, and if we know it, we can understand it. And if we understand it, we can fix it. Fix what? Well, the way we think. The remarkable thing about this therapeutic model is that we presume to end up someplace different from the mire in which we begin.

Psychological reflection can help for some. It's a start on self-inquiry, but too much of it further conceals, not reveals, who we are. It conceals us by giving us yet more erroneous self-concepts: new labels for phony notions of what we are and what we aren't, and from these concepts we construct what is laughably called a *comfort zone*. The walls of this zone are the limitations we set for ourselves, the beliefs we hold inviolable, the ground we will not bridge, the no-ways and the no-hows. We pad the inside of this cell with familiar habits and preferences. *That's just the way I am*, we say, to end the conversation. *Get used to it.*

I'm laughing about this because my comfort zone is never anything but damn uncomfortable, and so is yours. There's no room to turn around in it, no room for company or kindness or forgiveness. No room for anything new. Barely room to breathe. There was no happy girl in my comfort zone, but there was in my photo album. Somewhere deep in my skin was the capacity for untarnished joy and freedom. How could I find it again?

This is the question we ask ourselves nearly every day. In the asking, we make happiness a mystery: an elusive pursuit, an incomplete project, a scientific inquiry with inconclusive results. And yet the more we search, the farther afield we stray. The more we question, the more we doubt.

Happiness is not a science, an art, or an outcome. It can't be quantified, procured, or consumed. It's not invented, but comes naturally made from mud and honeysuckle, pitted olives, and doting granddads who hoist you into their laps for a bumpy ride on a secondhand tractor. It's what we are when we are utterly ourselves in unaffected ease.

Happiness is simple. Everything we do to find it is complicated.

My counselor suggested I buy a bottle of Old Spice. It was a brilliant suggestion, and I went to the drugstore, twisted off the cap, and inhaled my grandpa's blue work shirt and black lunch bucket.

I had a hunch there was more to it, something more than the resurrected memory of cinnamon and cedar. I had a hunch I'd been shown a more lasting family secret years before by a teacher who had never failed to see the real me — facing the day in a fearless way, sitting in silence side by side.

CHAPTER 5

Final Rinse

wringing out what's left behind

i'D ALWAYS MISTRUSTED the mean little black pillow he sat on when he turned his back to meditate, mornings and nights. Once I had tried the pose beside him, only once and only to please. Cross your legs and sit up straight. Follow your breath. Count to ten. I didn't get it. It hurt and it was dull, almost impossible to do, and who would want to? So when he chose it, day after day, a sacred routine, I tiptoed past, politely petrified that this peculiar thing would draw and keep us apart.

We came apart anyway, my one true love and me, and that's when a slender red spine caught my eye on a night spent roaming through what remained on the downstairs bookshelf. I opened

35

a page of the ancient Chinese verse the Tao Te Ching. I hadn't put the book there; I couldn't even pronounce the name. But the words fell inside me, dropped all the way down and echoed back up again. My skin shivered. My heart throbbed. Outside, a sudden wind raked a magnolia branch across the window, and I knew what I would do: I took my bed pillow and folded it into a high square and sat on it. For five minutes. The cool space that surrounded me seemed so significant that I wrote the date down in a book by my bedside: June 18, 1993.

"I feel dignified," I wrote.

Turned out he'd left quite a few books behind. About the Tao, and Buddhism, and Zen. Intoxicated, I downed them all like Jell-O shots and bought new ones. The man at the yoga studio told me the pillow was called a *zafu* and it cost thirty-six dollars. I left work at lunch and bought my own hard black cushion. Almost every night after, I sat on my cushion and watched the wall, measuring the time and my intent. *What am I hoping for? Why am I doing this?*

Deep in my gut a natural-born hope had bubbled up, but it wasn't hope for something. It was hope for nothing, a purge of ulterior aims and motivations, a clarifying rinse of all residue. I was finally reading the label, following the instructions I'd been given, arriving at the life I'd been handed, on my way to nowhere else.

There's a lot of misunderstanding about meditation. In fact, that's pretty much all that meditation is — the process of seeing how very much you've misunderstood about it and everything else.

We might be drawn to meditation because we want more out of life and ourselves. We might want to be more centered, for example. More peaceful. More focused. More balanced. More patient. More mellow. More wise. More like my ex-boyfriend who liked to meditate.

These may be all the reasons we are drawn to meditation, but they are not the reasons we meditate. We meditate because there is a six-foot flame dancing on top of our heads. It has made us mighty uncomfortable for quite some time up there. We try to pretend otherwise, but have you noticed? We have a fire on our heads! It keeps crossing the containment lines! The temperature shoots up and we prance about, panicked, frantic, holding our breath lest we stoke the inferno, but it rages anyway. About the time our eyebrows singe, we might heed the call of rescue.

That's how bad it has to get. If meditation is one of an array of self-improvement options you are considering, you probably won't do it. By all means, try the ninety-minute massage first! Get the new wardrobe and the hair tint! Meditation is the option of having no other option, no higher goal, and no more righteous intention than saving your sorry ass from a living hell.

This is why I was so fortunate to have smacked headfirst into Zen meditation — against my wishes and contrary to my better judgment — right there on the center shelf of the built-in bookcase by my own back door. Because in Zen, you see, we don't meditate on anything. We don't meditate on world peace, for instance, or loving-kindness, or forgiveness, or to acquire any of the lofty virtues that we or our dastardly neighbors so glaringly lack. Meditating on something else would just stoke the conflagration up top. We might be reminded — as if we needed reminding — of what we don't have, how we don't act, what we don't like, who said what to whom and how lousy we feel because of it. We meditate instead to quench the flame on our heads, to quiet the torment and silence the roar. That alone brings salvation, peace, love, and forgiveness. How? By itself. We have a wellspring of all that within us, a deep and eternal aquifer of fire retardant, when we give ourselves the breathing room to find it.

That's what we do in Zen meditation, or *zazen*. Breathe. Simply breathe, attending to our own breath as it rises and falls, fills and empties, counting it from one to ten and all over again just to give our brilliant brains something to do. We do this with our eyes open, looking at a wall or the floor in front of us. It's easy to think we don't know how to do it, and easy to think we're not doing it right, but this is the way to see that thoughts like that are just — oh yeah, look at that — thoughts, and we start counting again.

"Imagine that your nose is two inches beneath your navel," I read in one set of instructions. That may not be an appealing picture in your mind, so don't picture it in your mind. Don't picture it, and you'll immediately learn something amazing about yourself. Just by hearing the words, you automatically release the cinch in your belly, and your breath instantly deepens and slows down. For all the wayward searching for truth and authenticity in our lives, breathing is the most original, authentic, and autonomous thing we do. You know how to breathe, and only you can do it.

"I feel dignified," I wrote after my first solo attempt at sitting still. For the first time in what seemed like forever, I felt a breeze waft over my head. The breeze was my own breath. The breath was my own life. The dignity was my birthright.

Meditation is misunderstood because it doesn't look like anything happens in those torturous few minutes of motionlessness. But everything happens when you meditate. Whole worlds are dismantled, innumerable scores are settled, grievous deeds are undone, and the entire universe settles at rest.

Most of us say about ourselves: "I have a hard time letting go." Exhalation is the most complete expression of letting go, and we do it without thinking thirty thousand times a day. You know how to let go, and only you can do it.

"Ankles and knees hurt afterward but my mind and heart are collected and calm," I wrote when I had worked up to seventeen minutes.

Meditation is misunderstood as something you envision in your head, when in fact it is something to be seen with your own eyes. What you begin to see is that the place where you thought your life occurred — the cave of rumination and memory, the cauldron of anxiety and fear — isn't where your life takes place at all. Those mental recesses are where pain occurs, but life occurs elsewhere, in a place we are usually too preoccupied to notice, too distracted to see: right in front of our eyes. The point of meditation is to stop making things up and see things as they are.

When I give meditation instruction these days, I ask students to lift their arms up to eye level, wiggle their fingers, and see for themselves. That's where your life is, that's where your life has always been, in front of you, and now you know how I got mine back.

"I'm ready to stop asking questions and just accept," I wrote after three weeks of sitting myself down for a few minutes each morning and night. It was hardly the case, because the questions inflame me still, but readiness to be ready is no small breakthrough. Readiness is what lifelong meditators bring to their cushion, even when there is nothing left to bring.

Only when our hands and head are empty do we discover what we've been aching to find. The treasure is always intact within us, revealed in the final rinse. But please, don't take my word for it: seeing is the only worthwhile way to believe. I'm no religious scholar, but the sum total of Buddha's teaching seems to me to be just that. *See for yourself.*

With the clear focus of my open eyes and the strength of my steady breath, I was ready, yes, ready to see what would appear before me.

"This is getting interesting," I wrote about my ruined life at the time. I no longer had a home. I had no furniture. I had no love and none in sight. I had no pharmaceuticals. I had no plan. What I had was a mean little black pillow, a zafu, which had transformed into a cushion of kindness. I carried it with me like the ticket to a front row seat, convinced that when absolutely everything is washed away there's still something to see.

CHAPTER 6

Spin Cycle
changing the ending

ABOUT A QUARTER MILE UP THE TRACK, a runner approached me head-on.

I didn't run often. Heck, I didn't run at all. But since this was Thanksgiving morning in my first season of dislocation, and I had two dinner invitations, both hungrily accepted, I was inclined to overcompensate. I dove in with the die-hard crowd running a popular loop around a city golf course. Thankfully, I didn't have to go far before the clock stopped cold. The runner passed and left me astonished in his wake.

I braked and turned with certainty, leveled my voice, and called his name. First and last. I called to him twice, then three times.

He walked slowly back toward me with a glance at his watch. I felt suddenly idiotic. He looked at me foggily and relaxed his jaw into a wide and welcoming grin. "You look wonderful," he said.

He was tall and blond. A college swimmer with bleached yellow hair and a chlorine-scented tan. We were inseparable for three years, three years tending to be the limit on inseparability. And then he met me on the sidewalk between morning classes in my junior year and wished me luck.

It had seemed forgettable in the fifteen years since. But when I threw myself and everything else out of the big house, I took a stack of letters with me. They were his letters from the summer we'd spent apart, nearly one a day, dozens of envelopes of plain white dime-store stationery, saved because they had been my only love letters. *Love being what we called it*, I thought. I remembered the missives as mere training diaries, a log of swimming distance and carbo loads, unsatisfying to me even when they'd arrived, in dutiful succession, on unbearably hot and lonesome afternoons in June and July. After college, I'd seen him twice, accidentally, since we worked in the same city. He was married with children. I wasn't curious.

When I moved into my new place and carried the conspicuously bow-tied letters into the shared apartment, my roommate was randy to read them. One night for grins I dealt us each a stack. Inside was what I expected — grueling details of swim strokes and diet — and what I hadn't expected: his repeated assurances of love. My recollections had been stingy.

Seven days after that, I went for a holiday run and somehow put the story back in motion. He was the runner who passed me; his was the name I called. *Was it the power of my own mind? My memories? His words? The paper unfolded? The chronicle retold?*

There was a red light blinking on my machine when I got home later that night, stuffed from a second turkey dinner. His voice sounded eager and apologetic. He was so sorry if this was the wrong number, but if it was the right one he very much looked forward to a call back. I dialed and he answered, relieved, and sorry to be in such a hurry, but he'd looked in the phone book and taken a leap. He was sorry if he seemed too bold, but he'd already gone out and bought a card and sent it to my office, and perhaps I'd consider having lunch soon.

His wife had taken the two girls and all the furniture one day in September, and he was sitting in the hollowed-out house where the rest of his life used to be.

We had lunch, then dinner and dates, two tentative friends. I was reminded of what I liked about him: his innocent effort, his nearly awestruck attentiveness. In tandem, we moved ahead. We went running after work, I met his parents again, he met my friends, he picked me up from the airport after Christmas.

He turned to me in the frantic times when he most feared losing his children. I asked him questions he had yet to ask himself. I saw that he still carried a snapshot of a happy family now torn in two. The family hadn't been happy. But in the picture they were. He wanted it back together again.

Before long, we admitted to each other that we'd been imagining the same thing. A wedding day, with impish daughters and maiden nieces before incredulous guests toasting a wonderful-looking bride and groom who'd taken the long way around before reuniting in a perfect ending.

Is this how the story would go? The story that we tell ourselves to make sense and comfort out of chance and uncertainty? The story that hardly commands a shred of our immediate interest except for our constant preoccupation with how the story ends? To reassure ourselves that we know where we are headed and how everything fits?

That story. The trouble was, I no longer believed in that kind of story, or in my ability as a storyteller. My counselor had broken it to me, discreetly pointing out that the story of my tragic love affair was largely my own fiction. "In a relationship, each party has a story," he said. "A relationship breaks when there is no longer congruity between the stories."

In my current scenario, I could sense incongruity arising. How about when the story you make up is more enticing than the people you cast in the script? I wasn't in love with my old flame; I was romancing a story, again. Still spinning that sentimental song.

> It's still the same old story
> A fight for love and glory
> A case of do or die.

We're all inclined to do this, and yet we do it at our own peril, because when we insist on viewing our life as a story, we persist in repeating the past. The past is all we have to work with! Relying on familiar instincts and conditioned by past experiences, we inevitably end up spinning ceaselessly in a very sore spot. Delusion.

The bottom had fallen out, the walls had collapsed, and the curtain had closed on part of my life's drama, and here I was reenvisioning the future by looking over my shoulder. Who from the past was going to fast-forward into the present, I kept wondering, to obediently read the lines I'd written for him:

I've made a terrible mistake.

I've never stopped loving you.

I'm back to stay.

It never worked out that way, because life isn't a story, leastways not my story.

It's not your story, either. Quiet the narration in your head, even for a moment, and see for yourself that life is *life*, and not one minute of it is a retelling or a foretelling. Some things happen; some things don't. That's what makes it all worth seeing, no matter where it goes or how it ends. There is no spinmeister steering it to a foregone conclusion.

Even at my age, I still have friends waiting for a storybook partner, anticipating a storybook ending, trying to coerce uncooperative facts into fiction. Do you suppose we chase after commitment from another because we fail to commit to ourselves and our life as it is?

As far as my page-turner went, the momentum slowed. Weeks

passed without contact, and I called him to set up dinner, suggesting the time and place. When he picked me up, I turned to him sitting behind the wheel of his minivan and asked what was new.

"She's getting married," he said, he couldn't wait to say, with a rush of unveiled anguish over his ex-wife.

I settled into an evening of consolation, realizing that of all the things either of us needed now, "we" was not one of them. When he walked me to my door, I kissed him on the cheek and wished him luck, a bookend to the story I was leaving well behind.

CHAPTER 7

Hand Wash Cold

waking up to what it takes

THE TAXI DRIVER WAS AS LOST AS I WAS. Not exactly lost, but not where he expected to be. I sat silent in the back while he retraced the turns and then stopped on a narrow street crowded with pastel apartment houses and faded cars. Airport fares didn't come to this part of LA. I paid, grabbed my duffel, and stepped out.

It was a ragged neighborhood not far from downtown. Tiny bungalows perched behind chain-link fences; noisy, messy lives were on full view through open kitchen windows. Only if you looked up, straight up, at the palm trees swaying against the perfect sky, did you realize that this was once paradise.

I was unsteady after the big trip. And disappointed. A three-hour flight, and I was standing on a painted porch without a soul in sight. The door was locked. I rang the buzzer and an intercom voice answered. "Come in," the woman said. "We've been expecting you." The automatic lock unlatched.

Inside, the greeter handed me a retreat schedule and the keys to the room I'd be sleeping in for three nights. I nodded at all the instructions but couldn't respond, taking in the cases of books and papers and mismatched furniture that filled the room. "How nice you'll be houseguesting with Roshi," I heard her say, and I flinched at the rarefied name of the teacher I still hoped to avoid.

There is a place in our lives, should we be blessedly misfortunate enough to find it, where we can clarify once and for all the subtle difference between hope and trust and faith. The place is not one you'd ever want to end up in, but we all eventually do, and that's when we see we've been standing on this precipice all along. In the Zen world, this precarious spot is metaphorically called "the top of a hundred-foot pole." We are instructed to step off of it. Our hope doesn't help. Trust does. We take a step.

And that's how we arrive at faith. Forward motion.

"I'll take you to meet him," my guide said about the luminary teaching this beginner's meditation retreat. I stepped forward and followed behind, trusting that my toes could intuitively tread where fear would never set foot.

I'd gotten here the long way, maneuvering around my cynicism and ricocheting off self-doubt. My life was a sham, I'd been telling myself. My so-called meditation was fraudulent, a phony means to a dishonorable end. Couldn't everyone tell I was only trying to win my boyfriend back?

That's when I remembered his reverential reference to a teacher in Los Angeles, Maezumi Roshi, one of the first Japanese teachers to bring Zen to America, and now one of the last originals remaining. He was a real teacher, the likes of which you might confidently aspire to study with "someday" but hardly ever "today." From a safe distance three states away, I had dialed directory assistance and asked questions. When the woman at the Zen center said they had a beginner's retreat in a month, I said sign me up, because the date coincided with my birthday, and just then I'd begun to believe in magic.

Besides, I was imagining it would take place in a big room like a lecture hall where I could sit in the back, unnoticed, and judge everything for myself.

We exited the office into a shaded garden, and I had a better sense of where I was: amid a collection of modest houses and apartment buildings painted a uniform pale yellow with blue trim, covering about half a block. We crossed the backyard to the far house, which I took to be the teacher's.

Inside the door, we stooped to remove our shoes and then padded through the downstairs in stocking feet. In the living room, a little Japanese man, bald-headed and smiling, sat with two guests. My escort pulled up and did a short bow. I mimicked, stiffly. She made the introductions, adding after my name the qualifier "from Texas." He nodded, and we continued up the stairs.

I settled into the guest room. I was early, entirely too early, and where I thought there would surely be something, something important, to do, there was nothing to do but quiver and wait for the first sitting period, which would begin at seven that evening.

This was what Zen Buddhists called a *sesshin*, or a meditation retreat. Four periods of seated meditation a day, two hours each, divided into thirty-minute periods, with walking meditation in between. Meals, chanting, work, and rest filled all the other hours, starting at four in the morning and ending at nine at night. I'd been warned that, even though this was a beginner's retreat of only three days, it would be the hardest thing I'd ever done. But these days, everything was hard. Eating was hard, sleeping was hard, speaking and making sense was hard.

I lay down and listened to the street noise barge through the open windows. Cars, buses, horns, shouting, the forlorn refrain of an ice cream truck. I was too afraid to cry.

Shortly before the start, I put on my loose black pants and T-shirt and went downstairs to walk over to the *zendo*, the meditation room. It wasn't anything like a lecture hall. Wide open and nearly empty, with about thirty people sitting on cushions along the perimeter walls, I wouldn't be overlooked, but I could still be inconspicuous, or so I thought.

Just outside the door, Roshi, now in his black robes, stood with his attendant. They looked at me and smiled. "Are you ready for me to torture you?" Roshi kidded, the words softened by his accent and his laugh.

"I do that well enough myself already," I joked, flush with the narrowness of my escape. As we all knew, I wasn't joking, and there was no escape.

There was another joke I used to tell about myself. "I don't go anywhere they don't have valet parking." Only it wasn't a joke, and there was never any parking. I could never find a cushy style to which I could accustom myself, no sheltered spot to wait it out, no matter how relentlessly I searched.

From the standpoint of the ego self, which is easy to recognize as your judging mind, life seems to come at you like a continual inconvenience or, at worst, a massive invasion. We try to dodge the bullet. To get by unscathed. We situate and orchestrate, map, plot, outsmart, and engineer. All this fruitless effort is undone by the simple fact that our life does not occur outside us. It is not separate or even an arm's distance away, not on a shelf or a drawing board, never in a parking garage. It can't be entrusted to a valet driver because it never leaves our hands.

What's more, when we stay awake and focused on what is immediately obvious, the here and now, life never demands of us more than we can handle. It is always easier done than said.

We don't believe this, however, unless and until we prove it consistently by the sheer marvel of our being. Over and over again. This is why the single instruction I remember most enduringly from my encounters with Maezumi Roshi is: "Your life is your practice."

I was standing in the middle of my bare-naked life, and there was no escaping it. I'd have to do things the hard way, by myself, because that's the only way there is to do things. Step-by-step. Little by little. Read the label and follow the instructions.

Hand wash cold, it says. Line dry. More work than you'd like, but worth it if you ever hope to wear the damn thing again.

Months earlier when I'd started meditating on my own, I'd taken up yoga as well. The studio owner gave new students an orientation and invited us to ask questions. I asked only one: "Who was your teacher?"

He said the name of a famous author whose bestselling paperbacks were on my own reading list. He hadn't studied with that teacher; he'd read the books. I didn't know the answer I was looking for when I asked the question, but I do now.

A book may teach, but a book is not a teacher.

A teacher may find fame, but a teacher is not a celebrity.

A teacher comes from a line of teachers and completes a length of training that he or she freely admits is never complete.

A teacher is rarely found and yet astonishes you with his or her complete availability.

A teacher doesn't ask much of you — not your life, not your loyalty, and not a high fee for a once-in-a-lifetime opportunity.

A teacher waits.

By nine I was back in my upstairs room, the first night done. I'd followed everyone else's moves, a half beat off, responding to corrections whispered by well-meaning strangers.

The sitting had been easy and quick. Then I'd shuffled off with the other newcomers early for a lesson in eating *oryoki* style, in unison, using monk's bowls with chopsticks and chanting, all choreographed like a mealtime ballet. Come breakfast I would be lost. Nowadays I see that the discomfort of a retreat like this is intended to ensure that you do, indeed, get lost.

It was a strange night in a strange place and I didn't sleep, which wasn't strange at all. I was haunted by the terror of my fall. *Where, oh where, have I ended up?* I wrapped my head in a pillow to fend off the all-night noise from the street below and gradually sank into the wide-eyed defeat that accompanied nearly every night's tossing. Hours evaporated before I heard a gentle rap at my door.

"Kalen. Kalen."

It was Maezumi Roshi, calling my name to wake me up for the dawn sitting period. He said the *r* in my name like an *l*.

There are a few things you can say about meeting a master.

First, masters will never call themselves masters. *Zen master* is a construct of the English language and a sign of our insidious addiction to status. *Roshi* means simply "old teacher." There are many self-titled masters, and a number of roshis, but very few old teachers. You will know the difference on sight. A true teacher is likely to be the most ordinary person you'll ever meet.

In his baggy khakis and T-shirt, under a wide-brimmed, sweat-stained hat, Maezumi Roshi might have been mistaken for a gardener. It wouldn't have been a mistake. He was a gardener. In his threadbare clothes and modest quarters, he might have been mistaken for poor. It wouldn't have been a mistake. He kept himself impoverished. With his whisper-soft voice and heavy accent, he might have been mistaken for inscrutable. It wouldn't have been a mistake. What he said could not be grasped by the intellect, no matter how smart you were.

It was an unmistakable meeting with an unshakable effect.

I had come to this place in tatters, with hardly a shred of self-image intact, no poise or pretense. I was transparent. And so was he. But his transparence was brilliant, warm, and generous: it was the power of pure presence without the filter of a false persona.

In times of peril such as the time we now live in — when we are crazed by rage, uncertainty, and fear — spiritual thirst rises up. It's the same thirst humans have had through all of history, but the need quickens when our sense of security is stripped. These conditions create extraordinary opportunities to explore the truth and an equal number of opportunities to be exploited.

People are by nature cautious, so I'm often asked the best way to choose a teacher. It is a reasonable question, and the same question I asked Maezumi Roshi on one of the later, frequent, occasions I came to practice with him. Now I see how comic that must have been: sitting face-to-face with a teacher, asking how to choose a teacher. He responded sincerely, and so I'll do the same. He said, "Choosing the wrong teacher is worse than having no teacher at all."

As long as we are in the realm of choosing — using our discriminating thinking to evaluate what we like and what we don't, what we deem to be right or wrong, best or worst — we are not yet trusting our life or where it has led us. The teaching, after all, is to stop second-guessing the way things are. Your teacher is simply the one standing before you. That being said, I will offer other signposts, because where I was relieved by the sense that I had no choice, you may be confounded by the feeling that you have many.

Choose a teacher who practices what he or she preaches. Teachers can be charming, entertaining, and provocative, but if you base your choice on anything other than the vigor and authenticity of their practice, you will surely be misled.

Choose a teacher who has time for you and a practice center you can get to, or your spiritual life might be little more than intellectual tourism. You can find lots of information and opinions on the Internet, but these will never take you anywhere new. As long as you view yourself as a dabbler, you are holding yourself back from the wholeness you seek.

The teacher you find reflects your own sincerity and aspiration, so you will always get the teacher you are looking for. There is no end to spiritual entrepreneurs eager to trade your dreams for schemes. Sadly, there seems no end to seekers who sell themselves — their capacity and commitment — so short.

Finally, you will have your own hunch about all these things, and it will be right. An ancient master said, "I do not say that there is no Zen, but that there is no Zen teacher." You must trust yourself in all endeavors and have the faith to put your feet in motion.

Many things would happen in the years following this day, my thirty-seventh birthday. None of them were expected, but all of them were on schedule. Two years later, Roshi would die. Ten years later, I would ordain. Fifteen years later, I would write these words as if beginning the day brand-new. I would never again leave the laundry to anyone else, nor believe it could be finished once and for all. Immediately and forever after, my life would organize itself around a different axis: this ancient practice of ordinary life.

My motivation was a deep and insatiable desire. I wanted what he had. Easy laughter. Steady feet. Peace of mind. To be washed completely clean and ready, always ready, for wear.

I rinsed my face and dressed, went downstairs and out back, and sat in my spot on my cushion in the dim light of the zendo.

The room filled to stillness, and the timekeeper struck the bell three times to begin the sitting. Before long, Roshi and his attendant rose and walked out, turning down a side hall to the *dokusan* room I had been shown the night before, where the teacher saw each student in a private interview, sometimes more than once a day. This was the real stuff of Zen, I knew. The eyeball-to-eyeball encounter that revealed all. And this was the tight spot I still hoped to opt out of, unready to defend my feeble reason for being here.

The attendant returned to the zendo and announced that the dokusan line was open for those attending their first sesshin. The words were still foreign, but the meaning was obvious. *Me.* Right now. My legs responded and I stood, picked up my cushion, and watched my bare feet move in autopilot across the parquet floor. This was how I found myself kneeling in a shadowy hall waiting to show myself to the person often called the greatest living Zen master of the twentieth century. *Against my will.* I craned my ears to listen for the next cue recollected from last night's hasty lesson. From inside the interview room, Roshi rang a tiny bell, signaling me to enter. I stood, walked, stopped, bowed, went inside, and closed the door behind me, guessing at the moves.

Inside, I bowed again, a full prostration with my face to the floor, then lifted from the waist and stayed seated. Roshi sat two feet away. I spoke as I'd been told, stating my name and my practice, which was counting my breath. I didn't tell him that I didn't really know how to do it and doubted whether I did it at all.

"Are you a teacher?" he asked. His eyes shone black.

No, I wasn't a teacher. I had my own business in Houston, Texas, a public relations business for more than fifteen years, although I was going to sell it and change my life and all of that. And all of that.

"And you came to Zen by...?" he went on.

Not by my parents, and not by my education, not by anyone in particular, not that, no, no reason at all. By a book, I half-lied to no one who believed it, ashamed that an endlessly broken heart could send me tumbling all this way.

He nodded and talked. Kept talking and saying things I would not remember or ever repeat, streams of words assuring, encouraging, and appreciative, and I felt my face hot and wet and realized I had been crying for some time.

"You're not sitting quite *light*," he said, and I knew how true that was. He asked me to turn sideways, and he touched my shoulders so they lifted, showing me how to relax my neck and lower my chin correctly. He was slowing down now, winding it up. "Do you have a question?" he asked in courteous dismissal.

"Yes," I seized, aiming to do my best. "When I get up right now, do I do a standing bow or a full bow?"

He tossed his head back, laughing, and called me sweet, and I caught my breath at the nickname only one other had ever called me. "Smartness alone isn't as nice," he said. I stood and bowed and left the room, walked back to my seat in the zendo, awake and now fearless, moving forward to a practice place every one of us can call our own.

The kitchen.

PART TWO

the kitchen

To Study Oneself
Is to Forget Oneself

CHAPTER 8

Full Sink

who made this mess?

THERE IS A CERTAIN HOUR EVERY DAY, although it rarely lasts for just one hour, when I most want to leave home.

I see the faint blush of morning light under my eyelids. It's dawn. I hear the dog begin to patter on the parquet in the next room. It's time to let her out. I feel the inescapable weight of the morning routine descend upon me. It's time to get up. My husband sleeps on, undisturbed. It's up to me to do it.

There is the dog to attend. I let her out and fill her bowl. The coffee to make. I grind the beans and boil the water. The breakfast to assemble. I slice the fruit and toast the bread. The grumpy daughter to wake and marshal through her morning's grim reluctance. The lunch to pack, the clean dishes to put away, the dirty ones to load. The million, billion pieces of everyday freight to clear through this port, the kitchen, where I stand like a sentry over a long, dense shadow of never-ending duty. I am the stationmaster of this mess, and there's no replacement in sight.

There is an hour every day when I most desperately want to leave home. And the thing is, I should. I should spend the rest of my life leaving home, just by stepping into the kitchen.

Life is a kitchen.

When I say that, I don't mean I spend *a lot* of time in the kitchen, although I do. I begin and end every day there. Still, some folks spend more, and some folks spend less. Either way, that's not the point.

I don't mean my life is *like* a kitchen, although it is. I take the ingredients I have on hand, mix and mash them into the semblance of a meal, and try to nourish myself and others the best I can. I may not always like the taste of my own cooking, but I've learned that I can toss the leftovers out and start over. So yes, life is like a kitchen, but that's not what I mean, either.

I mean life *is* a kitchen, and when you do not yet see that your life is a kitchen, you may not see your life clearly at all. You are here for one purpose: to serve. Serving others will fulfill you as nothing else will.

I didn't come to this observation knowingly. When I began to rebuild my broken life, there were a few things I knew for sure about what I wanted to be, and this job was not in the description. Once imprisoned by property, I never wanted to own another home. I would be free and nimble. Having lost in love and marriage, I never wanted to entrap myself in a meaningless match. I would welcome love's first sight but forgo its aged fade. And seeing how fragile, frightening, and unpredictable the future could be, I was more certain than ever that I would remain childless. How could I give life when I had hardly savored my own?

I thought these deductions sounded reasonable and, based on what I knew about myself, smart.

But in every way, I ended up in some other place entirely.

How can this happen, we might wonder, when we have come to believe we are in command of our life? So sure of what suits us? Confident that we need only set a course to make all the right turns?

We are fairly convinced that visionary goals and intentions, executed with brand-name calendars, software, seminars, and positive thoughts, will deliver us to total fulfillment.

Except that's not how fulfillment works. It doesn't work the way we think or the way we want. Oh, it seems to sometimes, those few times the plan falls in place, and then we prematurely congratulate ourselves on our self-made successes. But most of the time it doesn't work, and we bemoan our complete failure to achieve the dream we had in mind.

But we do neither: we never fail, and we never succeed. We are not the designers of our lives. Life is the designer of us. Life is vast and grand, intelligent, clever, and completely unknowable. It always has the last word. It is the last word. Life interrupts us when we are at our most self-assured. Life diverts us when we are hell-bent on going elsewhere. Life arrives in a precise and yet unplanned sequence to deliver exactly what we need in order to realize our greatest potential. The delivery is not often what we would *choose*, and almost never how we *intend* to satisfy ourselves, because our potential is well beyond our limited, ego-bound choices and self-serving intentions.

I once read a testimonial from a woman who was trying out the "law of attraction" in little ways throughout her day. It seemed every time she applied the technique at her favorite shopping center, she found a choice parking spot. You know, the kind you never get. It feels good to find a parking spot. But then I thought, "Why doesn't she just give the parking spot to someone else and feel really good?"

And there's the secret. True satisfaction lies outside ourselves. It requires forgetting ourselves, along with our small-time schemes and narrow imaginings. Lasting satisfaction comes not by redesigning your ego's home according to your fickle predilections but by leaving that home entirely. True love demands the same.

"You've managed to have it all!" friends sometimes gush about the turnabout in my life. They don't realize that I have what I didn't want, and I manage it by not managing it at all. The only thing I try to accomplish, every day in the vicinity of dawn, is to open my eyes and take care of what I see in front of me.

"Let's just see how it goes," Maezumi Roshi would often say

in parting. I was an eager and impatient student in the early years, anxious for him to transport me to the promised land of an altogether different life. I could picture it perfectly.

It would be in a foreign country, yes that's where it would be, my different life. My face would be serenely unlined and radiant. I would, naturally, lose a little weight. My body would be lithe, no, make that skinny, from macrobiotic purification. I'd spend my days raking gravel and trimming candlewicks. Leaving my modest straw sandals outside my cell each night, I'd sleep in pious solitude amid the whistling hush of the pine forest boughs. I'd be like all the other monks — because there would be other joyful, impish monks — except for my hair. It would be long and lustrous, and, get this, after ten years of chemical coercion, it would reveal its own true nature: rich caramel brown with soft blonde highlights and not a sliver of gray!

I romanced myself by reading memoirs of Buddhist nuns and backpackers. Can you be romanced by such things? Yes, if you have an idealized notion of what constitutes a sacred life.

"Let's just see how it goes," Roshi would say as I pressed my suddenly urgent spiritual agenda. What do I do next? Where do I go now? When he responded with such seeming disinterest, I heard his dismissal as a cliché, a simplistic social courtesy. *He doesn't speak the language.* But that wasn't so. What he said was never mere social convention but was instead a precise prescription for enlightened living.

It always goes, you see, this life of ours. It goes the way it goes, moment after moment. The point is, do we see it without blinding ourselves with our preconceptions and biases? Without rejecting the unexpected or pursuing the ideal? The search for greater meaning robs our life of meaning. The pursuit of higher purpose leaves us purposeless.

The world doesn't need another wanderlusting soul seeker. The world needs a homemaker — me — to make my home within it.

Five years after my awakening to this once-unseen dimension in life — *the way things are* — I found myself fully equipped with nearly everything I'd once decided to do without: a house, a husband, a child, a dog, and a full sink to empty several times a day. Every day, I found my daughter's scorned breakfast left on the table, and my husband's crusty oatmeal bowl on the counter. I found streaks on the windows, crumbs on the rug, and footprints on the floor. I found shelves of food that no one but me would cook, cabinets of dishes no one but me would wash and put away. I found a near-empty milk jug, overripe bananas, and moldy bread. I found out the same way you did that a self-cleaning oven absolutely never cleans itself.

In all this mess, I found the ingredients for the next stage in the spiritual journey: the opportunity to move beyond myself and into compassionate care of everything and everyone that appeared before me morning, noon, and night. I found myself in the very heart of life, an ordinary life, the best spot to give and receive pure love.

You won't see it on a plan or a map, but I can tell you how to get there. It begins when you have the courage to leave home, and it leads no farther than your very own kitchen.

CHAPTER 9

Broken Glass

cracking the illusion of security

d INNERS WERE DIFFICULT. No matter what, dinners were difficult, while the days took care of themselves.

I had learned as much on the very first night, when I looked in the guidebook, called ahead, and walked a short way up a narrow Florentine street to the place where they held, ridiculously, my reserved table for one. I felt conspicuously incomplete as I entered the restaurant trailing a plume of empty space. The tables were crowded by parties of four or seven or twelve, loud and laughing groups, whole and happy families, while I sat insulated in my own dirigible of hushed air. I ate, paid, and discharged myself to bed.

This was not how it was supposed to be, this trip of a lifetime to northern Italy, the ripened hills that had awakened a thousand years of passionate appetites. I should have been accompanied. I should have been accompanied by a man, preferably younger and fashionably bohemian, someone who would stir my fearlessness. As fantasies are prone to do, my imaginary companion had failed to materialize. I had taken the trip alone, egged on by friends who believed I should do it to commemorate another milestone: my thirty-eighth lousy birthday.

Days were spent in and around famous places: the Duomo, the cathedral that swallows the city whole; the Pitti Palace, with its forsaken majesty; and the Forte di Belvedere, the southern mount from which all of time splays out in postcard panorama. One afternoon walking back toward my hotel, I stopped on the Santa Trinita Bridge to admire a blushing sunset and rainbow. Twilight traffic traced the river Arno's eternal curve. People hurried by me. I watched it all, uncertain of what to watch for. What was it, really, that brought people here? What was so special about a certain place or time? What transformed life into love? Had I missed the turn?

Soon, I would have to brave the evening meal. The book I'd borrowed from an acquaintance back home had the names of restaurants penciled inside the front cover. I chose one, Le Quattro Stagioni, eyed the map, and realized the restaurant was just a block across the bridge on which I stood. I headed on to see.

The place was tucked into a corridor of tall and darkened buildings, not a spot you could arrive at unaware. I entered its narrow and deep interior, yellow walls warmed with age, cozy and inviting to those who ventured inside. The maître d' took me into the far room and seated me against the back wall, a special spot for single diners, I gathered, because I was sitting nearly shoulder-to-shoulder with another single diner.

It was a woman. A very old and small woman, her hair wintry white, her face creased, her hands bent and bony. She was finishing her meal when she turned and smiled and spoke in a gentle accent.

"Are you Italiana?"

"No, I'm an American," I responded, pleased to have prompted a second guess.

The woman cupped her hand to her ear and leaned toward me.

"I can hardly hear. I'm over eighty years old!"

"But you're so beautiful," I said. Surprisingly, I meant it.

"I was," she said. "I won prizes."

I quaked to full attention. Here I sat in a restaurant named for life's seasons, another pathetic year beyond my summer's glistening youth, entering midlife's mystery, suddenly someplace I'd never been, with no one, no hope or promise, and an oracle had spoken. When would I finally seize this fleeting life of mine like a trophy in my hands?

I ordered a plate of crostini, bite-sized toast topped with tomato relish. Skimpy fare even for someone who didn't eat.

Soon, the woman rose and hobbled on a cane to leave. Passing by, she reached down and cradled my chin in her hand.

"Sweetheart," she said, "good luck and good appetite." And she left.

Minutes later the revolving front door turned again. A dark-haired man in a white shirt entered. I watched the waiter lead him in my direction, into my room, into my corner, into the old woman's still-warm seat, eyeing me all the while, making clear to me, at least, the main course he was serving.

I was afraid I knew who this man was. I was afraid I knew who had come to have dinner beside me. I was afraid I knew, but for once I knew I wasn't afraid.

He was my future husband, of that I was scarily certain, although I knew nothing more about him than that. It would become my repeated resolution to keep it that way. To know nearly nothing of him, and to expect nothing, for the long life of our marriage.

When we think we know someone, you see, we are already halfway to disappointment, and no one needs a head start on that.

This is not how we have learned to choose our partners, is it? This is not how we greet people, is it? With an open mind? With an eager hand? Like an unopened gift? Not when we make a life's work out of finding and keeping the perfect mate, the ideal match for our economic aspirations, political views, religious preference, height, weight, taste in coffee, and wardrobe sensibility — all the ways we foolishly seek in another mere validation for ourselves. When we believe we know what's good for us, what's right, and what we're looking for — and believe me, we all do — we condemn all our current relationships and doom the ones to come.

At this moment, I had no idea what I was looking for. I wasn't even looking. For what seemed like the first time in my life, I was truly alone, no longer appending myself to a love story. No longer trying to reconstitute a partner from the past, no longer imagining a fairy-tale future. My guiding impulse, as I studied the shadowy profile in my peripheral vision, was simply this: *Oh, what the hell.*

From that vantage point, I can assure you, anything can happen.

"How's your crostini?" he asked.

I invited him to have a taste. And you know what happens when you have a nibble. Before long, you've cleaned the plate and gone back for seconds.

In some sense, this was the most dangerous thing I'd ever done. It wasn't the first time I'd flirted. It was the first time I'd flirted without the slightest trepidation about how it would end. I suppose that's why it hasn't — not yet, anyway. It's the things we fear that chase us down, that haunt and hobble us until they inevitably overtake us and leave us with the weary self-fulfillment we were so afraid to find. *I knew this would happen.*

Fear is our first and, if we're not careful, our last love. It is our most enduring relationship. It never leaves our side. It tells us where to go, what to wear, what to say, and what not to say. We surrender all other options to it. Before, after, and during most of our relationships, we are concerned above all not with the other party but with what we fear he or she will do. Let me count the ways.

> I'm afraid I'll be embarrassed.
> I'm afraid I'll be disappointed.
> I'm afraid I'll be hurt.
> I'm afraid I'll be left.
> I'm afraid I'll be alone.
> I'm afraid I'll be unloved.
> I'm afraid I'll be taken advantage of.
> I'm afraid it won't work out.
> I'm afraid of change.
> I'm afraid to live.
> I'm afraid to die.

When I tell you that fear is the basic ground of ego, the false sense of a separate self, you might conclude what I do. We are unavailable for any truly loving and fulfilling relationship as long as we are trapped in a committed relationship with the most controlling part of our own mind — our fear. Our fear of what will happen and our fear of what will not.

Nearly everything we're afraid will happen is going to happen anyway, so what's to fear? There is no secure or unchanging ground, and we make ourselves safe only when we see and accept the way life is. Utterly spontaneous and impermanent. When it is time to laugh, we laugh. When it is time to weep, we weep. We are cheated of nothing in life except that from which we withhold ourselves by ego's narrow bounds. These bounds were made to break; indeed they must, if we ever hope to be whole again.

I'm not proposing that you play fast and loose with your self-respect, just that you abandon the lost cause of keeping yourself securely fixed in one place. It can't be accomplished while you are alive, and I can't offer an eyewitness account of what comes after.

During the dismal stretch of time I was wearing my big broken heart like a signboard, a flashing hazard light, a friend gave me a carved wooden heart. It was big, painted pink, and hewn from a single piece of pine. But the wood was too green. It was insufficiently aged, because the heart was nearly riven in two with a crack wide enough to see through.

"Is it cracked, or is it open?" she said pointedly when she gave it to me.

"How has he managed to stay alone for so long?" Maezumi Roshi asked me when he heard that I'd landed a good-looking forty-year-old American bachelor from Los Angeles on my pilgrimage to Italy.

"He wasn't alone," I said. He'd had any number of relationships that, like mine, had gone wrong.

"Oh good, then you will heal each other," he said.

He must have meant the kind of healing that happens when a blister pops and bleeds, when skin burns and flays, or when a fracture is rebroken to set it straight again. The kind of healing that keeps hurting as we break with our fearful selves over and over again.

I have broken many things in my second marriage: plates, glassware, door hinges, a wristwatch, and a heart or two, all flung in fear and frustration at not having my way. It's a habit I keep vowing to break.

A year after that first dinner in Florence, a rabbi wrapped a goblet in a table napkin and set it on the stone floor at our feet. My new husband shattered it with one stomp.

"Mazel tov!" the crowd around us cheered. It was a fitting benediction, the starting blast, for a lifetime promise to break up with myself.

CHAPTER 10

Sanitize Option

what children do not require

STOOPING TO MY KNEES, I reach into the cabinet. This is my nightly genuflection to receive my daily absolution. Under the eerie overcast of a fluorescent kitchen light, teetering on thin timbers of fatigue, after the last feeding and before the midnight cries, I put a tall pot of water on the stove and light a high flame to boil it. I squeeze a dozen six-ounce plastic bottles one by one between stainless steel tongs and submerge them in the churn. Then the nipples and the lids, five minutes at least, but I'm not counting the time, because time no longer counts. I want to do what is best no matter what it takes.

My baby is three months old.

I boil another batch of water. This is for mixing the formula, two scoops of powder into each bottle, topped by cooled water to the mark. Powder because it is cheaper than liquid, bottles because I have already settled for what everyone knows is much, much less than the best. I have settled on the substandard because my baby, born early, is too little and weak to nurse to her satisfaction, and by that I mean to my satisfaction. It is too hard, breastfeeding. It takes too long. It hurts too much. It produces too little. We have been roundly defeated and unsuccessful from the start.

When the bottles are assembled and shaken, I line them up in pairs in the refrigerator, an honor guard at the ready for another difficult day. Every day is difficult, although I have a pretty good hunch I'm making the days harder than they need to be.

The municipal water supply is safe; the label said the bottles need only a soapy wash and dry. I could fill from the tap and skip all the sterilizing, even catch some sleep. Still, I take measured comfort in the extra inconvenience: slavish compensation from my undue care. Nothing less will pass. It is my penance for imperfection, you see. Doing the most is the least I can do to win back the superlative ground I've already lost.

And then one night I see it: a button on the control panel of my dishwasher. An elevated half-inch, up to now unnoticed.

SANITIZE OPTION, it reads. Perfect. Bottles, lids, and nipples go in a basket on the top rack. Scientific, secure, certain. With one touch I believe I've found what a parent spends long days and nights searching for: the right way.

There are many things said by many people about parenthood; written and read about parenthood; counseled, debated, researched, and preached about parenthood — and too much of it has been by me. None of it is necessary. Not even this. So why do I write it? Because it can take a very long time to realize what is not required. I'm still hard at work on what doesn't need any work. Parenthood.

No other experience brings you so instantly into complete and inexpressible union with the divine. Nothing else is as genuine or encompassing. Nothing is more alive. No love is fuller; no intimacy, greater. Sex is close, but it's not even close.

Nothing compares to being a parent. And yet, all we do is compare. Most of us think, for instance, that we should be much better parents than we are. We infer that there is such a thing as a *good* parent, and by our own critical thinking we ensure that we are not. For when we judge ourselves as inadequate parents, we judge our children as the inadequate result. Judgment conquers our divine wholeness and separates our inexpressible union into a dueling dichotomy of incomplete parts.

The oppositional labels we assign to our life — and to the *loves* of our life — cause separation and alienation. Yes, just by a word, or by the fleeting phantom of a word. Perfect, imperfect, best, worst, more, less, good, no good, right, wrong, early, late, not enough, enough!

Yes, well, we're only human, we tend to say in consolation, missing the point entirely. By merely forgiving ourselves for our perceived limitations and inadequacies, we still judge the job of parenting to be beyond us, indeed, to be humanly impossible. We must go farther and completely forget ourselves to see that there is no need to perfect the life that appears before us. It is already perfect *as it is*.

Once I gave what I judged to be a good talk at my Zen center about the extraordinary challenges of parenting. The parents in the room nodded in solidarity. Why, oh why, was it so hard to do it well, to do it right? Ours was the most difficult job in the world! The discussion wound on and on, going nowhere, until my teacher gave a harrumph.

"Even monkeys can raise their young!" he said.

"Raise them *badly*," I thought at the time, taking his comment to be little more than the rude evidence of his unique insensitivity. "He might have been a father," I reassured myself, "but he was never a mother!" Mothers, I knew firsthand, could be the unrivaled experts at doing difficult things.

Parenthood is without question one of the hardest jobs in the world, and there is no one harder on you than yourself. To be fair, we're nudged along in fear and self-doubt by an unending stream of experts who don't mind telling us that the way we feed, hold, handle, speak to, and sleep with our kids is downright dangerous, particularly to their future test scores. No wonder we wake with a groan each morning as if we'd spent all night being kicked in the ribs by a little monster.

"Stop the presses!" exhorts one reviewer of a recent parenting book. "Everything you thought you knew about parenting is wrong!"

Really? By whose standards? By what measure? I can answer that myself, and every parent can, because, whether we admit it or not, we're all aiming for the same bull's-eye: a perfect outcome. I can tell you what's wrong too. What's wrong is to stand over the hissing steam in a late-night kitchen as though you're going to get a better child to come out of a boiled bottle.

It's not just the experts who dole out the body blows. We do it to each other. Venture into a park or playgroup and you're surrounded by advocates for various parenting styles. Advocating what? Their way, of course. We hurt ourselves, too, every time we fix on one way as the right way. One bend, one blind curve, and the right way turns into the wrong way in a hurry. Perhaps we feel so inadequate as parents not because of what we don't know but because parenthood shows us the limits of what can be known.

As parents, we think our job is to create an ideal future — a happier child, a smarter child, a more successful child. It's a silly notion, isn't it? That we are supposed to shape something presidential out of what looks like seven pounds of putty in our palm. The pressure alone makes us feel as though we're doomed to fail. But this focus on the future outcome blinds us to the marvel that already appears before us. It's not putty. Babies aren't blobs. Do we ever notice, and trust, the wonder of life happening continually and miraculously by itself? Do we ever see how effortless life is?

In my second, midlife marriage, I had a hard time getting pregnant. And then one day I was. Suffice it to say, I didn't use my noggin.

Stricken with pregnancy complications, I found it hard to keep going until the day she was born. And then one day she was. All I did was get out of the way.

It was difficult coping with a preterm infant. And then one day she wasn't. I can't take credit.

It was hard with a baby who never slept. And then one day she did. Frankly, I slept through it.

One day — it seems like only yesterday — she rolled over. Sat up. Crawled. Walked. Spoke. Ate with a spoon. A fork. Rode a trike. A bike. A two-wheeler. Read. Wrote. Skipped. Made up a song. Climbed a tree. Boarded a bus. Turned a cartwheel. Played the piano. Delivered a monologue on a live theater stage. None of it was hard for me, to tell you the truth. Monkeys raise their young; my teacher's point was true. But they don't do it with the degree of difficulty we impose on the process by our ego-driven judgments and expectations.

We expect it to be the way we want it to be; and the way we want it to be is the way we call right. In other words, *my way*. My way is what you have before you have children. There is no right way to parent; there is only a right-now way.

Like it or not, this is the offering that children give us, over and over: right now. We reflexively swat it from their hands — *I can't deal with that right now!* — since we are, after all, busy strategizing their brilliant futures. They return with the gift again, in fresh packaging. Children always show us the present moment unfolding. Our full attention is the only thing of value we can give them in return. Good thing too, because it is the only thing that makes a lasting difference.

When you step outside your judging mind, the mind that picks and chooses what it sees as good and what it sees as bad, what it fears most and desires least, you see that raising children is not impossible at all. It is only impossible to judge.

That's the day that you look up and see what all has happened while you had your head stuck in a cabinet. Your baby grew up all by herself.

This is bound to be an unpopular view. The popular view is that parenthood is difficult because we are inadequately schooled and supervised. I'll grant that's part of it. But I was adequately schooled and supervised in Spanish, and I still can't speak the language. I can't speak it because I don't practice it. As a parent, I make the job more difficult because I don't practice doing it the easy way. *The let's just see how it goes way.*

Those nights standing over the stove, I might have thought it would all get easier when my baby was out of bottles, then out of diapers, then out of a high chair, then out from underfoot, then out of my hair, and then finally out of the house. It was always going to be easier some other day. But I never had to wait that long. It gets easier as soon as you get out of your judging mind — the mind that picks and chooses your way as best and regards all other ways as less.

And what a happy day that is! When we liberate ourselves from the idea of parenting success, we liberate our children from failure, all without accomplishing a single thing. Freedom is instantaneous the moment we accept the way things are. Our own cruel judgment is what keeps us trapped over the stove long past the time when we should give ourselves a rest. And when we give ourselves a rest, we give everyone a rest.

I often speak to parenting groups with the aim of reassuring folks that they have everything they need to raise their children. It's a hard sell when you're not selling anything: not a lecture series, not an online class, not a packaged set of DVDs for $299. One of these talks was at a conference for parents of preschoolers where the workshops covered the usual rugged turf: handling sibling rivalry, effective discipline, nonviolent communication, how to raise girls today, how to raise boys today, resolving conflicts, teaching diversity, managing transitions, and a host of terrors that have us trembling in the sanctuary of our own homes. Leaving the hotel after, I saw a woman from my workshop sitting in the hallway crying, and I wondered if I'd done harm.

"You were the only speaker all day who didn't convince me I was doing everything wrong!" she told me. I urge parents not to be so hard on themselves, knowing that when they are hard on themselves they are hard on their children too.

But wait a minute, you might argue. Aren't we supposed to teach our children something? Instruct, direct, correct, persuade, dissuade, and convince them to think and act the way we want them to? There are plenty of opportunities to try all that, with spotty success. I rather like to think our children are here to teach us something: to give up and thereby gain the kingdom of heaven.

When my daughter was a year old — yes, a year! — I commenced a study of preschools. I gathered the brochures and made site visits. I compared the teacher-to-child ratios, the amount of shade in the play yards, the quality of the sand, the incidence of wooden versus plastic toys, and the pedagogy, and I ended up utterly confused. What I needed was a few hours a week to myself, and what I'd come up with was our first academic crisis.

My mother was visiting me at the time, and I laid out the prospects for her to deliberate on. Should I side with Montessori or Piaget? Waldorf or emergent curriculum? University laboratory or co-op? She spoke with the weariness borne of thirty-seven years as a classroom teacher and the clarity of a sage. "Karen, all that matters is love."

That's what children require. Not what we call the best, not what we think is right, not a push or a shove, but true love, love without judgment or condition, love for them as they are right now and for whatever they become. And equal love for our fumbling, tumbling tutelage. Within this wide-open field of possibility, anything can happen, and all of it is called *play*, not work, and not the most difficult job in the world.

How do you love a willful toddler? A bossy kindergartener? An obnoxious teenager? Love is not the same as like. We love our children whether we like them or not, and let's face it, a lot of the time we don't like them at all. Unconditional love does not pick and choose. This love comes without judgment but not without action. Animated by love, not fear, and not paralyzed by preoccupation with a future measure of success, we act to correct and direct our children right here and now.

The best teaching is usually our own behavior. Taking stock of ourselves, we often find that the annoying, stubborn, and disruptive behaviors of our children are attempts to coax attention from us. Our attention lags, and they learn how to revive it.

When we focus on what is in front of us, what is truly facing us in a situation, we know what to do and not do. I'm never confused when I see my daughter reach up to touch the open flame on the stovetop; I'm confused only when I try to deduce some future impact on her performance. Since in the thinking about what to do we become terribly confused, I tell parents to stop thinking about all the worrisome what-ifs and just stay present to what is. Then, if we overreact, we can always say we're sorry. There is no right way to parent, but saying we're sorry is something we can all get good at.

"Mommy, I feel sorry for God," my daughter said not long ago, "because he has to create a million billion fingerprints!" And here I am complaining about making another bowl of macaroni and cheese. As far as I'm concerned, she can call the source of creation whatever she likes; I'm just glad she's taken the responsibility for fabricating the human race out of my hands. I can make a mess out of the simplest things.

After I located the sanitize button, I became accustomed to running the dishwasher twice daily, nearly empty, for the sole purpose of washing bottles on superhigh heat. I must have overdone it. One afternoon I detected an acrid undernote to the dense vapor that rose from its door. It was a fire, an electrical fire inside the dishwasher controls. My perfectly good idea had gone up in flames, and once the fire was doused, the dishwasher was kaput.

We didn't do without a dishwasher for long. But there *is* something I never let back into my kitchen: the jury. It's still out on my parenting. Now we can all grow up to be ourselves.

CHAPTER II

Scrape or Rinse

marriage on a plate

H E STUDIED THE MODELS, rated the features, and compared the prices. He did what he does best, and what I ask
him to do in circumstances like this. He ran the numbers, and
then he picked out the new dishwasher.

I was happy with the size (it fit), the color (it matched), and
the delivery in two days.

He was happy with something else. "The best thing is, you
don't have to rinse the plates," my husband said.

For the record, you have to rinse the plates. You have to scrape them to within an inch of their lives. You have to scrub them, yes, even though that constitutes a complete washing before you load the machine. And sometimes, you have to throw them. Things have to break. This is a marriage, you see. Something's got to give.

"When will you write about marriage?" I hate when people ask me that. I just don't know what to say. I've been looking at a blank page for months — all right, years — and I just don't know.

After the courtship, after the kid, after too many conflagrations to count, I just don't know how marriage is supposed to work. There are no experts in my house. More and more it seems to me that every question in life is *how*, and every answer is *do*. And do, and do, and do.

You can try tidy formulas and messy compromises. You can soak the splatters overnight and hope they loosen by morning. You can stick religiously to the nonstick surfaces, and after a while even those start to stick. You can try all the methods professionals recommend and you still have a mess on your hands.

I've never found an easier way around it, so let me save you from expecting to find it. Forget the advertised claims. Drop the romantic illusions. Let go of your cherished ideals, the hoped-for bonds held intact by lifetime glue. For a marriage to last, you have to scour it yourself every day until not a fleck of fettuccine is left behind and it gleams like a mirror beaming back your own reflection.

Then, put it in the dishwasher for good measure and go to bed.

I've noticed that how we load the dishwasher says everything about the difference between my husband and me. I have a system that I rather like. I put the plasticware and glasses on the top and the plates and bowls on the bottom. I use the prongs on the racks to prop things in place so that the blast from the sprayer arm reaches each piece. I don't put my stainless, restaurant-quality pots and pans in the machine, because the instructions said not to. So I wash them by hand. I wash a lot of things by hand. Like when my husband loads the dishwasher, I wash many things that come out of it by hand. I do it my way.

As you might have guessed, he doesn't fully rinse the dirty plates or cruddy bowls before he loads them, because the instructions said not to. He doesn't always use the prongs to prop things the way I think is right. He might squeeze a wineglass into the lower rack, crowd an oatmeal bowl beside it, and cantilever a stew pot over both. Then he might take the cutting board and put it crossways on bottom, against the door, so the blast from the spray arm bounces off, pulsing out the side of the machine and soaking the kitchen floor. He does it his way.

Miraculously, it works. In the morning, I take the dirty dishes caked with dried food out of the machine and hand wash them. The miracle does not occur in the machine. The miracle does not occur in the second wash. The miracle occurs when I don't say a word about it. It's not only what *I* do or don't do; without me knowing, he silently performs a million miracles himself.

Truly, the miracle of marriage lies in what we don't say, and deeper still in what we don't know. Marriage takes one dishwasher and two miracle workers.

Sometimes people think I'm telling them they have to keep a marriage together at all costs. Phooey! That's something else I never say, because nothing stays put, intact, and inert forever. I only say that you have to keep waking up and washing the dishes, rinsing away your unmet expectations and stubborn resentments.

That's what helps me see my marriage for what it is: not the roaring flame we ignited, not the seamless partnership we promised, not the friendship we fantasized, and not quite what we were thinking.

It's taken me a long time to admit that my husband and I aren't each other's best friend, although friendship has never been our lot. At the onset of our midlife, long-distance courtship, after that fling as frisky strangers on vacation in Italy, I was uncompromising about our prospects. "I don't need a friend in Los Angeles," I said on the phone from Houston, a fair warning about the biological time bomb that had sent me hurtling in his direction.

The bomb went off, and shortly after our daughter was born I spent a good bit of time assessing the collateral damage. Having a newborn is more than enough reason to break down and call it quits, but she wasn't the problem. While the baby napped, I parked myself in front of the TV to watch a hypnotic loop of *The Wedding Story*, which back then ran in repeats throughout the cable network's afternoon time slots. The episodes impaled me with doubt, because the real-life couples on the verge of their vows always had a dreamy sense of destiny, adoration, and friendship that was unlike anything I experienced in my own life. I worried myself heartsick. Did everyone marry a best friend but me?

My best friend was back in Texas, and if I called her and said I had a flat tire in the pouring rain in rush hour on the 405 freeway, she would climb on a plane with two umbrellas and a jack. My husband would more likely counsel me with a cool head while never leaving his engineering cubicle: "Call Triple A." My marriage was not the stuff of white-horse rescues. Of course, it never rains in southern California, and I didn't fall in love with a tow truck driver. You think my expectations were off course?

That was before I decided to give myself a break. It was before I decided that marriage — at least our marriage — wasn't about friendship at all. Come to think of it, why would anyone want to marry a friend? I have plenty of friends and I do not want to marry any of them. I want to go have coffee with them and talk about how my husband infuriates me. That's the place to bring it up, if at all.

No, ours is not a marriage of friends making nice. Ours is a marriage of adversaries making peace. I wonder if that's what makes this odd and uncomfortable convention so transformative: not that we marry our friends but that we marry strangers — indeed, opposites — and then remarry one another every day. Perhaps that's what creates lifetime peace, love, and harmony: the honest effort, not the butterflies and moonbeams.

"So you mean there's no reason to get married?" says a friend whose very ceremony I performed. She is stumbling, dazed and defeated, through the scorched earth of her fourth year.

"There's no good reason at all," I say. There is no good reason to make any of the promises we make, and that's where the magic occurs. Marriage is not a choice you make like picking the glass tumblers from Crate & Barrel that promise to be dishwasher safe. (Mine cracked anyway.)

Marriage shows us how flimsy and meaningless the reach of reason can be. It teaches us to go beyond what we think we can do — *we can do more* — and reexamine just exactly who we think is going to do it for us: *each of us, by ourselves.*

Truly, there is not much two people can share. My husband and I do not share the same opinion about many things, except certain U.S. presidents and Academy Award nominees. We don't share tastes in music or reading; we don't have the same habits; we don't favor the same religion; we don't have the same inclinations about money, except we'd both like the other to make more of it. It doesn't take very much self-awareness to see that it is impossible for two people to share the same point of view.

We seem to disagree just because we can. It's another mindless habit. In the split second after one of us speaks, there is a choice to be made: accord or discord? Acceptance or rejection? A nod yes or a shake no? What you do or don't do in that second is the source of all second chances.

When the going gets tough, he'll say something like: "If people could see the way you really are, they wouldn't think you were so Zen." That's one thing we instantly agree on. I remind him that I don't practice meditation because I'm someone better. I practice because I'll never be anyone else.

A marriage is a lot like a silent meditation retreat anyway. In both cases, you come face-to-face with the most unlovable aspects of yourself, your messy unpleasantness, your selfishness, and the panicked impulse to duck and run. Neither experience is anything like the honeymoon you signed up for. The point is to pitch all that out and stay put. With my meditation practice, I can see that I'm still a cranky person, but I try to be a kinder cranky person. One who says less but always says, "I'm sorry."

You know I've been married before, so you might wonder how the second time around is better than the first. Surely the first one was wrong and the second one is right? I've stopped thinking that way. It seems to me that we have the same fights, the same frustrations, the same salty tears, the same low-grade despair, and yes, even the same loneliness. I've stopped thinking that one husband is better and one is worse, or even that my husband is different from yours. Comparisons are inherently false, distorted by our own self-centeredness, and serve no one. Besides, the way we tell it, husbands can seem uncannily alike. After two, five, ten years, or more of cohabitation, we still complain about the toilet seat.

In the middle of it all, I remember that my husband doesn't claim to have a spiritual practice, so how could he see things as I do? In the middle of it all, I remember that I *do* have a spiritual practice, so why don't I try to see things as he does? I cannot find a different husband, but I can find a different me who looks at things differently, taking more responsibility and assigning less blame, appreciating the whole instead of dividing the parts.

Two people may not share many things, but the truth of it is, they can share everything.

I share my husband's humbling and terrifying love for our child.

I share his pride and satisfaction when he fixes the sprinklers, his fuming frustration when they need fixing all over again.

I share a refuge, until one of us turns it into a war zone.

I share the unpredictable ride in this life of ours: the fits, the fights, the glide, and the cycles. There really are seasons, and they really are different. Take care that you do not measure the autumn by the spring.

I share the shortening horizon and the coming certainty that we will need each other's strength and gentleness over the steepest ground yet.

I share the blanket of calm, the dark secret of sleep's mysterious company.

I share his glance, his twinkle, his smile, and his touch.

I share the love that is quiet, patient, and kind, the love that bears all things and surrenders its way.

I share a pot of coffee in the morning and a sink of dishes at night.

"Do you want me to load the dishwasher?" he asks, because he so often aims to help me out.

"That's okay, I'll manage it," I say and wave him off, so caught up in my own arrogance that I've overlooked the gift. I do not say what I mean, what I still mean after all these years, the declaration that serves us without either of us knowing quite how. So I say it here before the assembled guests.

I do, honey, I really do.

CHAPTER 12

Stacking Up

and nothing to show for it

Sunday mornings start with an overripe banana, because there is always one left behind, bruised black and ready to mash into batter.

Then I add more or less equal parts of dry and liquid ingredients. Satisfaction always lies in the masterful balance between more and less.

Water works well enough. Milk, too, if I have it. A squirt of lemon juice adds zest. Melted butter tastes better. Baking powder lifts. Eggs add heft. A spoonful of sugar does what sugar does best. Adding berries makes it gooey. Adding nuts makes it interesting. Adding chocolate chips makes everything else beside the point.

I make a lot of banana pancakes. I make them almost every Sunday morning from scratch or from a mix. For family or for guests. For a half dozen droopy-eyed girls after the slumber party I swear I'll never host again. For holidays or for any day, I stack them high and keep them coming.

No matter which way or how often I make them, I have nothing to show for it. Absolutely nothing. Not one crumb. A lifetime of pancakes, and they all disappear without a trace.

I never ask myself if it's worth it, and that's how I know it is.

The kitchen is a wonderful place to view the folly of life's accumulations — the search for status, worth, and fulfillment — because nothing is quite as gratifying to the cook as a piled-up plate that comes back empty.

Kitchen wisdom is the ageless and largely unappreciated teaching of monks and grandmothers. Eating is our sole essential consumption, and cooking is our one common charity, so you'd think the value would be obvious. Yet, like many, I gave cooking short shrift for the longest time. With a critical eye to the value of time and what I judged to be my higher talents, I didn't think meal preparation was worth it. Or rather, I thought I was worth more.

Cooking for two? Not worth it.

Filling the fridge? Not worth it

Sitting to dine? Not worth it.

Cleaning up after? Not worth it.

I cooked but one Thanksgiving dinner before I turned forty. I'll be the first to admit the wait wasn't entirely worth it.

I busied myself doing things of greater value that promised superior returns, or so I thought. Building a career. Earning a reputation. Accomplishing a mission. Doing what I thought would satisfy. Striving for power, position, and security, illusions that sifted through my hands by the steady turns of time and calamity. There's nothing wrong with working hard and doing your best. There's nothing wrong with making money and spending or saving it. And there's absolutely nothing wrong with eating out. But none of those things are worth it, either.

Nothing is worth the measure we give it, because worth doesn't really exist. It is a figment of our judging minds, an imaginary yardstick to measure the imaginary value of imaginary distinctions, and one more way we withhold ourselves from the whole enchilada of life that lies before us.

If nothing is worth it, why cook? Why shop and chop, boil and toil, and clean up after? To intimately engage yourself in your own life. To see the priceless in the worthless, to find complete fulfillment in being unfilled. And to eat something other than your own inflated self-importance.

"Honey, come here!" my dad called to my mother the morning of their first visit to my home in California. I'd left my way of life in Texas — my job and singledom — for this new and different one. What was *different* was that it was no longer different from anyone else's.

"You've got to see this!" he shouted, and my mother hurried down the hall.

"Karen's making eggs!" It's true. My mother and father both lived to see me make a pan of scrambled eggs. They lived a bit longer after eating them too.

I don't want to make too big a flap about the merits of cooking. I merely marvel at the everyday lesson of seeing a construction you so earnestly assemble vanish in a *pffft*.

My pancakes are relatively harmless; the most troublesome things we accumulate are the ideas of what will make us happy and fulfilled. They always leave us hungry for more.

Just think for a minute about the people we idolize — the momentary champions of sports, business, beauty, and reality TV; the athletes and talk-show hosts, actors, CEOs, overnight sensations, and the founders of Google. They still have marriage problems, weight problems, tax problems, legal problems, popularity problems, drug problems, health problems, paternity problems, plastic surgery problems, and hedge fund problems. Does anyone really believe that these demigods have a fix on satisfaction? How much success, how much worth, insulates any of us from the twin torments of inadequacy and impermanence?

Oh how we know it, and yet, can we free ourselves for even one day from our appetite for more? We can if we study the culinary secrets of monks and grandmothers. Not many of us do, and so we miss — or arrive tragically late at — the one meal our life is serving us.

In the Zen tradition, monastic training positions consist of the very same things we might reluctantly do at home every day — cooking, cleaning, and yard work — yet in practice they are positions requiring great depth and maturity. The cook is on the crest of the heap. Lives literally rest in his hands. Enlightenment comes down to a bowl of rice.

Whether the shelves are full or empty, the vegetables fresh or stale, the broth rich or thin, in Zen meditation we cook ourselves into a state of even-minded ease with things as they are. Tasks are undertaken not because we want to do them, or like to do them; not because we choose to do them; not because we have suitable talent, temperament, or ingredients; not for reward or appreciation; but simply because it is *time*. Without thinking, we engage wholly in tending to needs as they appear and, in this way, live with clear purpose and total fulfillment.

My mother's mother set her bread to rise each day before the sun had yet dared to dawn, wrestling two loaves into the oven before a shadow had stirred. She saved a handful of the dough to roll into the morning's coffee cake and topped it high with buttery streusel. By the time I tramped into her ancient kitchen on summer mornings, the air bloomed with the sweetly sour greeting of yeast. It was breakfast time.

Her house is now flattened, ground into the dust of the earth's eternal crust. She is gone and the time has passed. But what she fed me still ferments on my tongue, and I recognize my place and lineage. Having the good life can be so simple when you savor the one you have.

The other day I had a letter in my mailbox with a return address I didn't recognize. I let it sit a bit before I opened it while I ripened to fullness with its fragrant possibilities: the gushing thanks, the unexpected accolade, the irresistible offer that it contained.

I live this way a lot, squinting around the bend, anticipating what I'm about to get. Don't we keep expecting to get something? In particular, to get *it*? To figure *it* out? To reach a culminating resolution, reward, complete understanding, wisdom, clarity, closure, the right answer, the holy grail? That very expectation fills us up and weighs us down.

The letter was nothing I imagined. It was a note from a long-lost cousin lately relocated from Japan to the States. Another granddaughter of the very grandmother I've just recalled. She had adopted a daughter, and wouldn't it be lovely for our sisterless girls to each gain a cousin?

I cried at the long circumference of the circle.

She mentioned that she had a woodblock print of the Zen garden at Ryoanji temple in Kyoto. You might be able to picture it: the proverbial Zen garden with nearly nothing in it but granite rocks and raked gravel. The inscription on the print reads: "I am content with what I have," she wrote. No, not quite, she corrected herself, capturing the subtle depth of the teaching: "I am content with what I lack."

Looking for greater purpose, some people think that housework is beneath them. Cooking and cleaning is beneath them. I know that feeling well. Sometimes it is so far beneath me that I can't see the bottom of it. I can't see the beginning or the end. I strain to see the point. But again and again, I do.

It is the only work that truly enriches me, that cradles and supports me. For all its selflessness, kitchen work is an authentic expression of self-love. As I stand at the sink or stovetop, as I survey the listless lettuce in the fridge, the kitchen is not apart from me; the kitchen is me, and the life nourished here goes on well past the vanishing point.

At the end of the day, my counters cleared and dishes stacked, the big payoff appears. My sink gleams, empty, like a deep ocean pearl, and I am content.

Look for more and be dissatisfied. Look elsewhere and be confused. The ingredients are always on hand, and it's impossible to run out.

Having nothing to show is simply having enough.

CHAPTER 13

The Good Dishes

the life we're saving for

MY MOTHER SAT in the blue upholstered rocker and pointed at the glass-front cabinet in the dining room. She wanted each of her daughters to choose something inside, to agree on a division before the final dispersal got out of hand.

Preventing a future tempest was one last thing to tend to before time would overtake her. She was so shrunken now, so bony and frail, that just raising her arm seemed to supply enough forward thrust to lift her heavenward. As it was, her ascension wouldn't be long in coming.

Good days found her in the chair, from which she could view most of the corners in her tiny tract house. Bad days were spent in the hospital bed in the back bedroom. Her year of cancer had displaced the familiar and turned her flinty prognosis — no future to speak of — into an excruciating wait.

Her cache of collectibles was meager. Cut-glass bowls, etched stemware, and unused china. I didn't want anything. My mother had already given me everything I would keep, everything I would cherish. I hesitated, uncertain if this moment was for me or for her.

I finally nodded my agreement, like the stoic last bidder at an auction. She wrote my name in shaky script on a shred of paper, and I taped it to the bottom of a painted teapot that had never held a drop of tea.

In my kitchen cabinet I have a sleek cocktail shaker that has never stirred, four matching martini glasses rimmed with dust, a stainless steel kettle unused for fear of use, and a glass gravy boat that has been docked in place for over a decade.

These are not crimes; they are not misdemeanors. Serving gravy is not a virtue, although eating naked mashed potatoes could rightly be called a sin. Still, these things catch my eye, sitting pretty behind glass doors like curios, and I wonder from the deep trench of my fifth decade what in the hell I am waiting for. The guest I'll never host, the success I'll never toast, the turkey I'll never roast? How much of my life do I unwittingly set aside, hold in reserve, or postpone for lack of my own attendance?

These are benign reminders of the life I've failed to occupy, devoted as I am to saving up for the one day that never comes. Tomorrow.

"What day is tomorrow?" my daughter asks. She's three years old, and I couldn't be more pleased that she has learned the days of the week. It seems precocious, and more evidence of what I hope will be an accelerated future.

"Wednesday," I say.

"No, what day is tomorrow?" she asks again.

"Today is Tuesday, so tomorrow is Wednesday."

"But when is it tomorrow?"

I'm no longer sure what she is asking.

"It goes Monday, Tuesday, Wednesday, Thursday, Friday," she says, ticking them off. "But when is it Tomorrow?"

When is that day called "Tomorrow" that factors so eternally in our plans and schemes? I gape at her clear-eyed misperception, at her supremely intelligent confusion. How many times have I lost her in the mists of my ramblings about that never-to-come day? Everything, it must seem to her, is going to happen Tomorrow. And for good reason: it's where we adults live most of the time, straddling the yucky puddle of the here and now, teetering on our tiptoes to plant one foot on a better future. One we think we can control. It simply can't be done, and so we keep toppling over, face-first into our good intentions. We complain that our lives are out of balance, and wish we could one day learn how to live in the moment.

I hear a lot about living in the moment. I hear about how and why and when, and how hard it is to live in the moment. The truth is, there is not a single person on this planet who is living anywhere *but* in the moment. It's just not the moment we have in mind. The moment we aspire to live in is a different kind of moment, a better kind. A moment of solitude, perhaps, of quiet satisfaction, of thrilling accomplishment or satisfying retribution, of deep confidence and unshakable certainty, with children asleep and ducks lined up and ships come in and gravy, yes, that extra spoonful of gravy on top. *That's* the moment we are waiting to relish.

In the same way that we misapprehend "the moment" as any time but now, we misconstrue "the now" as any place but here. Calling it "the" now suggests a certain kind of now, a different now, a better, special-edition now that is attained by secret knowledge or effort.

It is the effort of lifting your eyelids.

No one has to master living in the now. It's impossible to live anywhere else. Just as you can never leave now, no one will ever take away your past or withhold your future. Effortlessly, your past accumulates. Instantly, your future arrives. What matters is that you notice your life while you can still call it "alive." That's now.

At least, it matters to me and my still-beating heart.

There's really nothing more to it. For your own peace of mind, get rid of any three-letter word that you might automatically insert before *now*. As in *the* or *not*. Take those out and put nothing else in. Get rid of the idea that now is anything but right here: where you are, as you are.

"Now" may not be all it's cracked up to be, but the real problem with it, I suspect, is that we think it's not enough.

I thought if I grew up, did my best, and made everyone proud of me, it would be enough. I thought if I got a good job, got a better job, made money, and then made even more money, it would be enough. I thought if I could lose ten pounds, get a better haircut, get the right jeans, then lose the same ten pounds, it would be enough. I thought if I could understand, explain, and express my feelings well enough, it would be enough. I thought if I wished, hoped, dared, or dreamed enough, then it would finally be enough.

Then I thought: *enough.*

I practice being enough. When I do that, everything is already enough, and this is the day I've been saving for.

A year ago the hillside behind my home was engulfed in wildfire. We anchored ourselves in shock and disbelief until we got the call to evacuate, then loaded up assorted papers, dusty photo albums, baby videos, and a week's worth of clothes. For her part, my then-eight-year-old daughter walked the rooms and declared without a scrap of sentimentality: "We might never see this house again." Choosing the few things she would rescue, she donned her pink Disneyland cap and her Girl Scout vest and met the moment bedecked with badges and pins, under a pair of mouse ears.

That precious glimpse was proof enough that I needn't look behind or beyond. We wear it all — the infinite past and the limitless potential — and it's inseparable from the way we are right now.

The fire was quenched that day and we quickly returned home.

One thing I didn't pack for safekeeping was my mother's teapot, because I don't have it. I don't know where it ended up. Like the moment that brought me here, I've never seen that teapot again. Just as well; my mother drank her tea ice-cold from a plastic pitcher she kept in the fridge.

But the other day, I looked into my kitchen cabinet and saw my own shiny stainless kettle that's been sitting unused on a shelf, and I put it on the stove to boil. I've saved enough. Now seems like the right time, the only time, to use the good stuff.

$\backsim$

Ordinary Life

love the world you wake up to

t HERE IS AN ODD INTIMACY in sitting side by side on the floor. No posturing.

The two of us hunkered down on the scratchy nap of our bedroom carpet, knees cradled, voices low. This was the moment that, over mounting years and in separate ways, we had feared most.

Earlier, I'd told my daughter about my decision and she did not react. It would take the actual experience, the real event, to trigger a response from her. I told myself she could handle it.

My husband recoiled at my news, clamped shut in his private loss.

On the stretch of rug between our closeted wardrobes, beside the double vanity, below the range of our reflections in the mirrored wall, I spoke into the darkening hours about how relieved I was to finally be free.

His shoulders lurched and the sobs came in heaves. He was losing the wife he thought he had — the look, the picture, the package — and I knew his pain as my own. I fell silent, the words incomplete, and reached for him across the space in between, where at long last I found love.

This was not the end of a marriage. This was the beginning of a buzz cut.

When I first began my Zen practice, I was finicky about my hair. I had it cut and styled expensively, highlighted religiously, and I blow-dried it into brittle submission before I bade the world hello. Every day I scrutinized my tenderized pate for shine, bounce, and fullness, and nearly always found it lacking.

I was still knotted in my topmost obsession when I began hanging out with shaven-headed monks at rustic mountain retreats. While they were contemplating nonattachment, I was wondering where the devil to plug in my 1,750-watt Conair. Deep below the scalp, I must have known where my head was headed. One night in a dream, I lifted up a silky tress and exposed what was hidden below: a bald knob as barren as a bowling ball. The vision haunted me, and I switched to a volumizing shampoo.

When we first married, my husband was finicky about my practice. He worried about what went on under the blanket of meditative silence for days and nights on end when like-minded devotees conjoined in bliss. He told me his nightmare: that I'd saunter off on one too many retreats and disappear for good.

Every bit of it came true, just not in the way you might think. Zen was the end of me, in one sense, and the beginning of everyone and everything else. When I committed myself to the priesthood, I didn't lose my family or my home life. I'm still here. I lost only my carefully constructed self-image, which was falling apart anyway.

This was never my life plan. What I planned was to stay young forever, stand pat, hold firm, have my way, and fight the good fight. The day I decided to ordain, and the night I told my family that I would shave my head, I felt the dead slag of self-consciousness crack open, the weight of ten thousand bad-hair days drift down to feathery piles at my feet.

Who is this self-image we defend to the death? Who is the one we name, the picture we frame, but a construct of yesterday's wishes and tomorrow's fears hammered together with incessant thoughts of *not good enough*?

I tell myself I'm not a good enough priest, for instance. I shaved my head as part of the ordination ceremony but have not since. I keep my hair about an inch long, sometimes closer to two inches. Those are two inches I don't need but from which I haven't yet disentangled myself. I make no mistake: that pinch is the distance between heaven and hell, the space between extra and ordinary, the last torturous trace before I leave my ego's crumbling house and come home for keeps.

It can seem like an impossible span: the divide between the things I clutch most dearly and those for which I profess to care. On the one side is self, with all my likes and loathings, and on the other, complete and selfless love. This is the love we call compassion for want of a word other than *love*, which contorts with a mere half-twist into hate. And oh how we love to hate.

The words *love* and *hate* are the product of the egocentric mind, our self-centered thinking, the home of our likes and dislikes. Egocentric self is the voice that pipes up and says, "This is good. I like this. I'm happy." Or that might say, even about the very same circumstance that once gave us pleasure, "This is not good. I'm tired of it. I'm not happy." The thoughts and feelings that originate in our heads do not last. Just taste the bitterness when familiarity curdles to contempt, and you'll know what I mean. The kitchen will give you plenty of practice.

When I was a kid, my mother gave me a whole bowl of whipped cream and let me eat to my heart's content. (I think she knew what she was doing.) I loved whipped cream, but I ate myself sick and never liked it again. The whipped cream didn't change. My view of it did.

Affection is fickle, but there is a love that lasts forever, and you'll find it when you release your grip on the self you cherish above all else. The love you'll find when you open your hands is compassion.

Do-gooders think quite a bit about compassion. We want to

have it, feel it, and do it, but compassion doesn't need doing. It exists already in the harmony of things just the way they are. Discord comes from our doing; compassion comes from undoing. It greets us when we undo our boundaries and erase the lines we said we'd never cross. Compassion waits in the space between us, the space that only seems to separate us: a gapless gap we close by reaching an arm's length in front of us to wipe a tear or wash a breakfast bowl.

We can only love the world we wake up to. The world where things change, dishes get dirty, we age, we get sick, and, one day, we die.

There is an urgent truth to life, and yet most of us spend every moment trying to hide from it. Our bodies will betray us; the chemistry will backfire; the oat bran won't be all it's cracked up to be. How many times will we fail to recognize, how many times will we overlook, how many fruitless attempts will we make to nip and tuck and camouflage the uncompromising need to make peace with ourselves, to make peace with time and life and death? How many do-overs do we beg for while trying to back away from life's ironclad contract? Someone has to make a change for good, and that someone can only be you.

You don't have to go as far as I did; you just have to go farther than you think. You can do it. There is no greater power than your own.

We made it through the hair thing. We made it through that night, and day, and the ordinary nights and days that kept coming. We lost nothing but a losing proposition: the illusion that any of us is what we appear to be. When it was time for the big reveal, my husband was sweet and sensitive about my bony head. Everyone was. My daughter was honest. "I don't like looking at your skull," she said, and so I covered it with a scarf to be kind.

After that, the world seemed a lot kinder than I ever gave it credit for. People look kindly at those who appear to be sick, as I did, and so I looked kindly back at them. For once unconcerned with my own appearance, I became more concerned with others. It took no effort. There's an eyeful right in front of your face. Often people look frightened and lonely. They seem bothered, hurt, and terrifically sad. Kindness doesn't cure everything, but it cures unkindness. What a magnificent place to start.

I don't wear my hair anymore, even the little I have. I wear a smile. I laugh a lot too. I'm unafraid to be unadorned and insignificant. Each day I do the dirty work, the effort that attracts no notice but my own, and in this very place I find the ordinary ingredients for genuine fulfillment.

It starts the moment my eyes open, as I rise with the sun to sort and stack the dishes, appreciating this simple task as the essential start to a healthy day. Chopping the blemished fruit into breakfast, savoring the taste of my own usefulness. Emptying full hampers without resentment or commentary. Making a marriage from sturdy pots and pans, an enduring masterpiece of mutual forgiveness. Cooking dinner while my daughter plunks the loveliest praise songs from the piano, knowing that my own mother, standing in her own kitchen, once received the same sweet cup of satisfaction from me. Watching my family circle each other in wary regard, wrestle, and shout a messy wreck of feelings, seeing them suffer their deep adoration of each other, and leaving it be, well and good and theirs alone. Keeping silent about some things and laughing about almost everything. Loving all of this, and then forgetting to add even that, so full to the brim with this life already.

I made a turn that night on the bedroom carpet, away from futile self-absorption and toward the world with everyone and everything in it. One little turn transforms a dreary patch into the paradise we share. I can't wait for you to see the whole of it.

PART THREE

the yard

∿

*To Forget Oneself Is
to Be Enlightened by
the Ten Thousand Things*

CHAPTER 15

Full House
no inside, no outside

tHE REAL ESTATE AGENT WAS CHATTY, a fount of commentary to drown out the disinterest with which we viewed our housing options. Two years married and as yet unsettled, we were looking for a house to rent, a spot to park our ambivalence about commingling our separate ways and starting family life for real: a place to finally grow up. In one overgrown backyard, she dangled a promise in lieu of any other attributes: "You might find the footprint of a Japanese garden underneath all this ivy."

My eyebrow went up.

She couldn't know the conversation that had preceded this expedition by four years, the lighthearted exchange that had predated our wedding by a year: the awkward introduction made just months before Maezumi Roshi's unexpected death. Meeting the man who would later become my husband, Roshi teased him about living in a quaint suburb of Los Angeles, a funky hamlet with an overblown name.

"I hear you've been living in Sierra Madre," Roshi said when he shook my future husband's hand, rattling our composure. "What are you doing living in that dinky little town?"

I was stunned. "Roshi, do you know Sierra Madre?"

He laughed. "I was a gardener there when I first came to America."

When the echo sounds, we might finally hear what we've been told.

Still, one cocked eyebrow does not a conversion make. We'd come to Sierra Madre to look, and so we kept looking.

"Let me show you this one just for historical interest," the agent said from behind the wheel as we approached another house. It had been a long and fruitless day. Perhaps we were tourists and not takers.

She braked to a slow cruise as she began the story of a bygone estate once encircled by three gardens, including this one — *we stopped* — now the oldest private Japanese garden in southern California. The empty bungalow beside it was added at midcentury, behind the rusty wrought iron fence and a thicket of giant bamboo, beyond a garden gate etched with a kanji inscription, "Mosses as abundant as ocean waves." I had goose bumps by the time we stepped inside the front door carved with birds on a blossoming branch, and out back, again into the garden, the welcoming arms of the garden, its ponds and rocks poised in place since 1916 under the shifting shade of century-old sycamores, the water falling in the hushed company of a silent teahouse, the pines pining, and each perfect plant waiting patiently for a gardener.

"The whole thing was built for Zen," the Realtor added knowingly, knowing nothing about me or how to judge the reaction that had frozen me in place.

I looked at my husband looking at me. I cried, he smiled, and we stepped into a story that was suddenly ours.

First I made you leap forward in the story, and now I ask you to step backward in the story, and all to show you that every journey is a journey to the same place. Across boundaries of false judgment, presumed barriers, and perceived distance to the very spot in which you stand right now.

Life is a garden.

When I say that, I don't mean I do *a lot* of gardening, although I do. I weed and rake. When they aren't providing shade, the sycamores I once swooned for drop a rotten load of leaves into my lap. Still, some folks do more and some folks do less. Either way, that's not the point.

I don't mean my life is *like* a garden, although it is. Seasons advance, each with its own rhythm and purpose. Winter rests, spring awakens, summer rages, and autumn warms its lonely bones with windswept memory. So yes, life is like a garden, but that's not what I mean, either.

I mean life *is* a garden, and when you do not yet see that your life is a garden you may not see your life clearly at all. You are the garden, you are the gardener, and you reap what you sow. What will you make of the ground that you — *only you* — can tend? How will you share the place you never leave, the time you always have, and the peace you alone can spread?

You make everything true by bringing it to life, so be careful what you bring. Anger kills, bitterness poisons, greed spoils, fear stunts, and inattention withers. Good gardeners cultivate a good earth. And where could that be but the very spot where you stand?

Of course, we want to occupy ourselves with improving the world *over there*, even if by that we mean the future world, the world of our children and grandchildren. It is a noble goal. But are we ever there? No. Your life, where you are, as you are, is the only paradise you will ever find. Stop judging it as right or wrong, good or bad, and you'll meet it face-to-face. Attend to it, and it will flourish.

No one could ever tell us if the garden we entered on that remarkable summer day was the one Roshi had tended when he first came to America. I didn't need anyone to tell me. Nor did anyone but me know that the citrus trees in the front yard released the fragrance of a happy childhood I would never forget: my grandfather's oranges. You always know when you've come home.

In spite of the time and distance, the yearning and roaming, we never leave the place where we belong. Still, most of us take the long way back.

How did this happen? I can't comprehend it. The plot is too far-fetched for my imagination. The map is beyond my spatial reasoning. Perhaps what the wise ones teach is really true. There are not two places. There are not two times. There is no inside and no outside. There is no past or future. There is only here now. Don't try to understand it, and you will understand it perfectly. You will see it, you will smell it, you will walk on it, and you will trust it, once and for all.

When I tell people the story of how we came to live where we do, they usually say one thing and mean another.

Incredible! *Nothing fantastic ever happens to me.*

Amazing! *I am a nobody.*

You should write a book about it! *My life is boring.*

Then I think about the dozens of people who tramped through this property before us and didn't claim the prize for themselves. It's easy to see why. We might have had the same fears and reservations, but my husband and I just went one step farther.

It's too much work. *We'll take it bit by bit.*

We might make a mistake. *Gardens grow back.*

Too few bathrooms. *There's room for another.*

You have to step through the gate, the false barrier of your critical mind, to see all the ways we habitually reject the very place our lives have landed us. And then, we have to stop plotting an escape. That's what practice is for: staying put.

Believe me when I say you already have what I have: the sun blazing in your heaven above, the rain falling on your head, the flower blooming under your gaze, and the moon that follows you wherever you go. You have the ten thousand things. You have everything inside, everything outside, and someone telling you they are not even a hair's breadth apart.

You have everything at hand. It's not an impossible task to make the world a better place. Indeed, it's an everyday job. Gardener to gardener, we start by simply taking a look.

CHAPTER 16

The Sun
attention is love

THE NOTE, penned in his shaky script, had come by mail. Everything about our yardman, Sam, was old-fashioned like that. His ancient van, a hulking eyesore he plowed into a cockeyed stop at the curb; his simple hand tools and bandannas; his spotted and stubbly face, weathered to an indeterminate age. Although I saw Sam every Wednesday, talked to him, worked beside him, and paid him, every communication came like this: handwritten on lined paper, addressed to the "Mister."

"The part will take too long. I'm sorry I cannot take care of garden anymore."

Sam had come to us through a nearby nursery, his name and

number on the back of a receipt when we asked the manager if he knew any Japanese gardeners in the area. Years after moving into our house with its splendid old koi ponds, yews, and pines, we were still looking for the expert who could tend it all. The knowing and wise master who could pare a bushy branch into a subtle brush stroke, sculpt a lumpy shrub into a poetic suggestion. So when Sam came, looking the part and charging nearly nothing, we gave him full rein.

We asked him to draw up a plan for the property's empty north side, a patch unkempt for decades. He brought back a primitive pencil rendering and a list of plants we should buy. We bought the plants and lined them up expectantly for his artistic installation. I watched from inside, first confused, and then aghast, as he plopped the plants into the dirt without rhyme or meter. When I saw him place the stately junipers at drunken, tilted angles, I went outside for an explanation.

"More interesting," he said.

I wasn't interested in that kind of interesting, and after he left I shoved the tottering trunks upright. It helped a little.

Sam was a lost cause, we concluded, as each week we found a tool or two he'd overlooked and left behind to rust. He didn't have a delicate touch. He didn't have aesthetic vision. The atrocities mounted, and we finally surmised that, behind his inscrutable squint, he might not see so well.

Still, he showed up, and the less we asked him to do, the longer he stayed. He spent hours in the sun fingering weeds to pluck from the mossy hillside carpet; passed cheerful days culling fallen leaves from the understory. He loved the garden, he loved the daylight, and we hesitated to take either away from him. When the note came, referring to an unavailable part for his broken-down van that had left him without transportation, we suspected another part, long failing and irreplaceable: *his eyes*. He couldn't see the obvious, and for the longest, neither could we. Sam was blind to the imperfections we saw, and, caught up in our preconceptions, we were blind to Sam.

Sam didn't teach us anything about Japanese gardening, but we learned from him nonetheless. Gardens, like children, are forgiving; gardens grow. Love, even clumsy and unrefined, cultivates. Time, unhurried, is never wasted. Today, looking out my window to the northside planter, I see the legacy of Sam's teaching. Roses sprawl in crowded bloom regardless of how precisely they were planted. The junipers grow heavenward, strong and true, toward the even and ever-present light. The garden is imperfect, but it is no less beautiful or bountiful. It thrives.

Without trying, Sam showed me one of the great teachings in the phenomenal world. Right in front of me, in plain sight, I had finally seen what the full sun can do. The sun gives attention, and attention fixes everything.

If you haven't noticed the sun, then you probably don't know what I'm talking about.

I mean the sun comes up every day. It is the hardest-working, most reliable, most dependable, most consistent, and most generous thing we know. It delivers the dawn, the days, the seasons, and within them, the mysterious internal combustion that triggers life and intuitive, intelligent growth.

The sun shines, always, blazingly full, illuminating through the overcast, shimmering through the haze, eradicating shadows, and overcoming, with time, all obstructions.

And it endures, in its infinite, replenishable power.

It does not demand; it does not impose; it does not withhold or revoke; it simply shows up.

This kind of presence — full, vital, and affirming — is attention. The sun attends the earth and everything in it.

When the sun's attention is in short supply, plants show it. They contort themselves toward the light, enfeebled, stunted, and unproductive, never developing into what they still contain the complete potential to become. They are attention-deficit disordered. We are all, in our own insidious ways, attention-deficit disordered. But like many things in plain sight, we usually don't see it. We aren't paying attention.

Here in our world, we have a curious epidemic, or maybe not an epidemic. It is overdiagnosed, or maybe underdiagnosed. We know how to treat it, or maybe we don't. We read about it, talk about it, and argue back and forth about it, but we can't seem to collectively focus on it long enough to find a cure. Too many of our children — and even late-diagnosed adults — are afflicted by attention deficit disorder. It is perhaps the only deficit that most of us will ever encounter. It seems to be rotting our families and ruining our lives.

Let me be the first to admit I don't know the first thing about how the brain works. Or the heart, the spleen, or the gall bladder. I'm not your go-to girl on medical mysteries. But I agree with most people when I see unmitigated torment and suffering, especially in children: *Someone ought to do something about it.*

That someone often ends up being someone like my cousin, a social worker. She works with the families of children who have severe emotional or behavioral problems: kids heading toward hospitalization or foster care. Her agency is a kind of last-chance depot on the road to disaster. You'd think that if your child, indeed your entire family, landed in these straits, you might begin to pay attention.

Although the consequences are extreme, the goal of my cousin's program and others like it is small, very small indeed, because even a small behavioral change can produce the margin of redemption. She sits down with a family at the start of a case and tries to winnow the whole catastrophe down to one change they can all work on together. One change to save everyone's life. What will it be?

"I want my child to stop interrupting me when I am on the phone!" said one mother, two mothers, a sequence of mothers and fathers, grandmothers, aunts, uncles, and overwrought caregivers, testifying to the distortion and disease that descend when the sun has been gone for too long.

Attention has been given a bad rap. Too much attention paid to a child has become something better off spared, like snacks before dinner or swimming on a full stomach.

"He only wants attention," we might snigger about the tantrumming toddler, the rambunctious youngster, or the rebellious youth. And then we often turn our backs, as though blocking the sun will force the wayward among us to straighten up and do right.

This might sound like too simple an argument, too naive an explanation. And most things in life are complicated. At least we think of them that way: full of contradictory causes and dilemmas, dueling sides, and irreconcilable differences.

So let's think of this in the simplest way. Attention is the most concrete expression of love. What we pay attention to thrives. What we do not pay attention to withers and dies.

What will you pay attention to today?

I tell people about how much time and effort it takes to be a wife and mother. About how it occupies my whole life. I say I can't imagine a time when I'll have more time, when my life will once more be my own.

In truth, I struggle daily giving even one measly minute of undistracted company to my family, and I'm here all day! When do we actually *have* the children we say we have? When are we actually in the relationships we're in? What portion of the years, the days, the hours of our lives do we spend being the people we define ourselves to be? Fulfilling the roles that we ourselves have chosen? Doing the only full-time work there is to do? How often do we do what Sam did, what the sun does, what everything everywhere does without a blink? When do we simply show up? Not very often, it seems to me now, even though I tell myself my family takes all my time.

We have replaced Sam with a small crew of gardeners who come for one hour a week. Quick and efficient, they make a clean sweep and leave nothing behind. They have many other places to go. And while the shrubs are all doing fine, it is up to me to put into practice the larger lesson that Sam has shown me.

If I encounter you on my way today, I'll look at you and say hello.

If the phone rings, I'll answer. If you send me a message, I'll respond.

When my husband opens the front door, I'll stop what I am doing to greet him.

When my daughter comes home from school, I will have nothing to do. We will have no reason to hurry. We will lounge on the floor or linger on the lawn. I will turn the computer off. When she speaks, I will listen, without steering the conversation to a conclusion. If she has a scheme, I'll go along, and let her pull me off course. We will let the hours lapse and the afternoon drift. When she looks at me, and even when she doesn't, I will embrace her in the shine of my smile.

Today, for a moment more than I think I can bear, I will give her attention. I will give you attention. I will give this world my complete attention. I will give it the time, the companionship, and the love that Sam taught me. I will give it the sun.

CHAPTER 17

At Hand

all the time in the world

THE SHADOWS SLANT. The light retracts. The dark sneaks in to steal the days.

I scan the sky, sniff the wind, and think, "It's early." In another week I'll think, "It's late."

From November on, I swing to sudden gusts the way a faded leaf twirls from a slender stem. Like clockwork: anticipating, estimating, when will it be? Waiting for the drop from the top to begin the slow sweep of the great heaps beneath.

How foolish to measure time by the rate or the date of gravity. In no time at all, it's always that time again.

Time to rake.

Time has ahold of us. You know, the time we're looking for. The time we missed. The time we're going to give more time to if we ever find the time.

The question I'm asked more than any other is: "Where do you find the time?"

So let's say a word about time. But let's not say what everyone else says. Let's not say, for instance, that time flies, or time runs out, or time waits for no man. Where do I find time?

I don't. I have never yet found time. Time isn't something we find, but time is something we lose, all those times we fail to recognize that time is always at hand.

We are never apart from time. This is not how we think, especially when we think that time is coming, or that time has passed; that time is the prize, or more often, that it is the problem.

Time doesn't even exist. *You* are what exists. Time is what you are doing at the time you are doing it. There is no time other than this, so stop searching for the perfect metaphor for time and pick up the rake already. It's time to rake, it's time to cook, it's time to clean, it's time to write, it's time to drive, it's time to rest, it's time to pay attention to how we use our time.

I often tell people that they have all the time in the world. They look up from their frantic scramblings, their scattered minds, feeling overwhelmed and bogged down, and they think, to put it nicely, *Get a job, lady.* What I mean is that there is no world other than yours, and you have all the time in it. Seems simple to me, but it's shocking if you've locked yourself in a losing battle for time.

We think of time as the enemy. An implacable patriarch exacting a toll, a swift second hand, a death march. What looks like time passing is living proof of the profound, true nature of all things: impermanence.

Life, we think, could be so much more, if only we had more time. When we view real life as a roadblock, we're held prisoner by time. Yet through it all, we're having the time of our lives.

I know the argument: *Easy for her to say! She doesn't know how much I have to do!* Yes, the to-doing is impossible. To-doing takes up quite a bit of time. Should-be-doing is a close second. Either of those could well be the principal occupation of our lives: imagining scenarios, planning strategies, reorganizing priorities, fretting outcomes, second-guessing choices, and then sticking the whole rigmarole back into the familiar rut that's so hard to get out of. *I'll tackle that when I have more time.*

Particularly these days, the thinking goes, the fast pace of our lives leaves less time than ever before. Not quite. Time management is a timeless practice.

A thousand years ago, a Zen disciple complained to a master about having no time. "You are being used by the twenty-four hours every day, but I am using the twenty-four hours every day," the teacher replied. Using it to stay present, that is.

How can you master time? Time management is self-management. Accord yourself with what needs to be done — the very thing that appears before you. What appears before you is not only the most important thing; it is the only thing, all other things existing only in your imagination, for the time being.

Of course, what appears before me might well be what I judge to be unworthy of my time: the work with no visible end, no redeeming value, and no apparent urgency. Is there wisdom in doing the work that we might rather overlook? Yes; it's called the wisdom of telling time.

The garden always shows me what time it is. In the fall, the broad canopy turns faintly yellow and the leaves sail down. First by ones, and then by tons, into the pond where they float and eventually sink, until I hoist a net over my shoulder and scoop out the muck that would otherwise displace the water itself. A part of every autumn day finds me fuming at the sight of falling leaves. Then, I get on with it.

Tell me, while I'm hauling leaves 'til kingdom come, is it getting in the way of my life? Is it interfering with my life? Keeping me from my life? Only my imaginary life, that life of what-ifs and how-comes: the life I'm dreaming of. *I am unable to accept my MacArthur Genius Award at the present time because I am scooping leaves from the pond.*

At the moment when I'm in the muck, at the moment when I'm doing anything, it is my life, it is all of time, and it is all of me.

In the spring, the garden bursts to life, and once again I see what time it is. It is time to weed. We used to enjoy having a carpet of scrub across our rolling backyard. I say *enjoy* but I really mean *accept*, because what, in the end, is more enjoyable than acceptance? Our vista looked perfectly green, but the ground was mostly weeds, and we left them there for an idyllic length of time.

Then, we thought better of it, landscaping the whole thing with mounds of grass called dwarf mondo: little plugs that can cover a big space. When I am weeding now, the mondo covers the whole of my world. I have replaced that sense of carefree disregard with the drive and agitation I imagine a surgeon feels as he surveys his daily schedule of life-and-death procedures. I am a backyard neurosurgeon, prying sprigs of weeds from between the delicate roots of my baby mondo, my vast and miniature world.

When I look up across the endless stretch of the job before me, I surely want to quit. *Isn't my time better spent elsewhere?* But if I manage to regain my focus on what's at hand, I realize it's just one weed. There's always just one weed to do next. I do it weed by weed, and the weeds always show me how.

I do things one at a time. It's the only way you do things too, but you might not think so. Perhaps like you, I once thought my life required me to multitask. Now I'm not so sure that anyone is a multitasker, although many people think they are quite good at it and even want to give people advice on how to become better at it themselves.

During the time in my life when I considered myself a world-class multitasker, I worked all the time, doing a lot of different projects with a lot of different people on overlapping deadlines. It felt like I was doing everything, all the time, all at once, but I ended most days feeling like nothing got done.

I suppose because we have more than one hand, we believe we can do more than one thing at a time. Like drive and text. But the brain doesn't work like that. We have only one brain, and it pays attention to only one thing at a time. The fact is, we are often so distracted, overstimulated, and preoccupied with our own thoughts and feelings that we aren't paying attention to much of anything at all.

Doing things one at a time doesn't mean I do them slowly. I do them singly. No matter what the job description, we all have just one job: to focus our attention on what is in front of us, and to let our attention go to work.

Nothing is accomplished except little by little; it's only that we judge some jobs to be bigger than others.

Sometimes the task before us seems so overwhelming that we sputter out before we've begun. We are already mentally rounding the curve toward the steep and sticky part, the complex, exhausting, immeasurable length of it, the part we can't imagine doing, and so we stop right there. These days, I try hard to stop stopping and just start starting, because every impasse and impossibility is just one weed, saying, "Pull here." Everything moves through this one place in time; the infinite and unimaginable totality of existence moves through this one moment of motion.

I don't ever finish. Like everything to be done in the garden — like everything in your life — weeding is something you start but never finish. Nothing stays put. Everything done comes undone.

We see this front and center in our lives as parents. Even

though our children change every day, we don't always notice. We don't notice until we clear out yesterday's clothes, and then — *snap* — how did all that time disappear? What seemed like forever is now forever ago. And all those special times we intended to have! All those precious moments we were counting on! We use a good bit of our time feeling lost and distraught, or even depressed, because time seems to take the upper hand.

I'm sure it can seem to some that all they have time to do is work, leaving all the other priorities to languish on the periphery. I hope for your sake that when it is time to work, all you do is work. But in those hours when the choice is truly yours, what do you choose to put in front of you? Where do you cast your enraptured eye? Where do you lose yourself? Where do you invest your time, your life, and your love, knowing that whatever you pay attention to thrives?

In the temple where I practice — and in monasteries, churches, and cathedrals everywhere — time is signaled with sound. Three bells to sit, two bells to stand, and a drumroll before meals.

When your time gets out of hand, I suggest you sound an alarm. Take a kitchen timer and put it in your hand.

Turn the dial, and when the bell rings, switch off your iPhone. Shut off the television. Power down the computer.

Turn the dial and, before the bell rings, take a nap. Read a book. Meditate.

Turn the dial, and spend one hour in undistracted company

with your loved ones. If you tell me that you don't have one hour a day to spend in undistracted company with your children or your partner, I'll say it's about time. It's always about time.

One night the moon was full and I lay awake for a long while. I went into my daughter's bedroom and watched her sleep. I saw through the deep shadows and the midnight glow. She did not stir.

I went because the nights are numbered and I do not know the count.

Days and nights come and go without end, appearing and disappearing into thin air. Notice, and you'll always notice what time it is. You'll always know what to do.

When I grow weary of what's undone or anxious about what's to come, I remind myself that I am not the maker or the order-taker in this life. I am this life, and it is unfinished. Even when it is finished it will be unfinished. And so I take my sweet time. Time is savored when you take it by the hand.

CHAPTER 18

What Dogs Do
when an object no longer offends

The Lord is my shepherd;

I shall not want.

He leadeth me beside the still waters:

he maketh me to lie down in green pastures.

He leadeth me in the path of righteousness for his
    namesake:

he restoreth my soul.

THIS IS NOT QUITE HOW IT GOES. I know it is not quite how it goes. I don't remember how it goes, but I mumble it anyway. It is the least and the most I can do.

Thirty-five years before this day, I won the Bible Bee at a summer church camp in north Texas. I was fourteen, a champion of rote versology, and Jesus had just become a superstar. But a new language was overtaking the familiar King James version of my spiritual upbringing, and I was soon knocked from my cozy throne. I still knew the stories, I could recite the laws and lessons, but the test questions had changed. Was I saved? That's what Christians suddenly wanted to know, but I was no longer sure by whose standards I qualified. I was not born again that summer. And when you're not born again, pretty soon it's all history.

Now standing by the bed in the ICU, the respirator inflating my father's chest like a pipe organ, I leave aside the Buddhist incantations that I've naturalized and whisper remnants of the old soul song. *I will dwell in the house of the Lord forever.*

I'm thinking that my dad would like it, should he still be able to do something as sentient as *like*, in this mechanical suspension before my sisters can arrive to make the last decision. By anyone's judgment, my father is a failed Christian and I am a forsaken Christian, except that in death, as in life, we are all one thing. Words matter in times like these, but not the words that once brought us to blows.

My father didn't love easily, and so he was not easy to love. For as long as I could remember, my mother ran interference for him. "Your daddy really loves you," she'd say. We all had reasons to doubt. As soon as I could steady myself on two feet, I kept my distance.

One time my two grown sisters and I reminisced about the good old days.

"What was your most traumatic childhood memory?"

"When Daddy kicked Karen down the hall." Both my sisters said it. I had no recollection, but I didn't need one to believe it was true. My father was the kicking kind. He kicked dogs and small things underfoot, a class of brute that surely doomed him to hell.

Life was plainly hell for him already. His was an unrelenting darkness without the grace of even one flicker of faith. After Mom died, my sisters and I would imagine his decline, certain that the burden would befall us to be kind to an unkind man and generous to a scrooge. We weren't at all sure we could do it.

In his loneliness, he had taken a dog, a rescue, although we hesitated to think Dad much of a hero. The dog was skittish and untrained. She wet the carpet many times a day.

And then things had turned out differently. My dad began to do things differently.

He imagined a new life in a new place, far away. He set about, with the intention and resolve he had lacked in nearly every other year of his life, to accomplish something. He gave away or sold all the stuff we were so sure we would be saddled with. He sold his home, the albatross we'd already hung around our necks. He loaded up his dog and his truck and moved to a mountain town where, six months later, he could no longer breathe.

There, looking at his pallid agony, the cruel limits of a life lost to pain, I cried and I smiled, realizing that only I could supply what had been so sparing between us.

"I love you," I told him just before we turned everything off. And then, to my sisters, "I'll take the dog."

That spring, my mother had come to me in a dream. Four years dead, she was standing on my front porch. I rushed up and hugged her. Her body was like ash in my arms, crumbling and decayed, but I was not afraid or repulsed. She took me up. We flew into space, into the vast darkness and pulsing light. I felt celestial wind in my face. It was exhilarating.

I asked her, "Is there a heaven?"

She said yes.

"What's it like?"

Like this, she said, like this.

It was an attribute of her deep faith and her final, modest confusion that my mother believed she was dying on Easter, and it was, for her. But for the rest of us it was in the small hours before Good Friday, the dark night after Maundy Thursday, the day commemorating the Last Supper, when Jesus gave his disciples a new commandment to love one another as he had loved them.

Not too long ago I chanced upon a telling of what has become a bit of family lore, that my mother, a devoted Lutheran and good churchgoer, had never known I was Buddhist. She would not have stood for that, the reasoning goes among my relatives, who had mistaken the strength of her faith for hardness. True faith is not hard at all. It is soft in its resilience, yielding in its certitude — the vehicle for absolute grace.

What is true for me, what I remember, is what my mother said when I told her of my first encounter with my Zen teacher and the peace I had found. What she said then was what I recognize today as the ultimate sanction a mother can give.

"Now I don't have to worry about you anymore."

In the dream, my mom brought me back to my own front door, and then she said something.

"There's only one thing I want you to do."

"What is it?" I would have done anything she said. I was filled with immense joy and thankfulness.

"Love Jesus," my mother said.

I will, I said. I will.

Only later, upon waking, did I wonder. And then I stopped wondering.

There are many names, many stories, but only one love, and only one place or time that I can love them all without exception.

I did not want a dog.

I am not a dog person. I am not a cat person. I am only intermittently a person person. In that regard, I have never been anyone but my father's daughter, unable to outrun his footsteps in the hall.

But I've learned that it takes a mother to heal a daughter, a daughter to heal a father, and a dog to heal us all. There is a shepherd's psalm to soothe in every wilderness, and this dog has brought me mine.

There were troubling signs from the start.

My husband flew to Denver, rented a minivan, and drove the dog, her blanket, her bowl, and her toys 833 miles to our doorstep. She catapulted from the car, darted through the front door, and peed on the Oriental. *No one should have to put up with this.*

And then, the hair. Clouds of fur drifted along the baseboards, coated the sofa, and clung to our clothes. Was it stress, allergy, vitamin deficiency, or climate change? Was it her food, water, flea treatment, or shampoo? We called the vet. *This can't go on.*

And then, the yard. Her pee killed delicate mounds of moss; her poop pocked the pristine footpaths. *What is that smell?*

And then, worst of all, the walks. I chafed at the bridle; I yanked at the leash. She bolted in front, chasing cats and squirrels, sprinting and vaulting, exposing my complete inadequacy as a handler. She loved it. I hated it. *I hate her.*

And then.

Little by little I shed my resistance. Like a lark, I've made a nest from never-ending dog hair. I quit pinching my nose and picked up a poop scooper instead. When my dog places her quivering muzzle on my lap telling me it's time to go for a walk, I release my selfish grip on the day. So many walks around the block, and each time I come home to a very different place, all because of what dogs do. They save your life by making you leave it behind. Good dog, Molly.

Follow a dog, or a horse, or an elephant, for that matter, and with every step you're brought to new ground right under your feet. You're brought to that new ground whether you follow anything or nothing at all, but these animals can help you notice it. If you detect a residue, a stain, or a whiff of lingering stink, you know perfectly well that you'd better scrape it off.

Just now, mired in the familiar stench of an old story, my dog, Molly, has led us somewhere fresh and clear. Do you see?

I love my dog. And that means I'll take the dad.

We have a saying in Zen: "When an object can no longer offend, it ceases to exist in the old way." It doesn't mean we just think of it in a new way, or assess it in a new and favorable light. In Zen, we always mean what we say, and then some. Eliminate your separate, self-reinforcing view, and an offending object ceases to exist in the old way. There is no one left to take offense. There is only love, the love that never leaves.

Life is all about love. I can't imagine what more there could be to it. We've all come here for love: to get it and to give it, there being no separation between the two sides of the transaction. Love is the reason we do everything, and love is the reward. Love is the spirit, and love is the form.

As sons and daughters, sisters and brothers, mothers and fathers, dog walkers and cat fanciers, we are all caregivers, and love is the care we give. Actually, that expresses love in a stingy way, as though it is rationed from one to another. Love is far more than that. Love is what we are, when we drop all the things that stand in the way.

The last night in the ICU, I felt my father's life recede and I lost my footing. I could not stand. I could not walk. The nurses wondered if I had the flu and suggested that I go to the emergency room.

"No," I said, "it is my father dying." They assumed that mine was an emotional response. But it wasn't emotional. It was real. I clung to my chair like a raft against the undertow. And then I felt, as never before, that my father was *me*, that altogether we were but one life, interdependent and inseparable.

When all was said and done, we turned off the machine and death came. I spoke prayers, verses, and encouragement, and I found out how easily I could. The poet is not wrong. *Surely goodness and mercy follow us all the days of our lives.*

So it turns out the dog is not difficult. She is even-tempered and sweet, uncomplaining, an ordinary dog.

I love her, but I do not love her as if she were something else. She is not my baby or my bane. I do not pamper or perfume her. I love her as a dog, true love allowing each and all things to be just as they are.

"She was my father's dog," I am quick to explain to others on first meeting, and then I stretch the unspoken for a moment after, because what I really mean is "She is my father."

By making a home for her, I've given abode to my father as well: reconciling difference, settling transgressions, allowing things between us to be over and done. Should I enliven old wounds with resentment or rumination, I only kick myself.

I can answer my mother and the others now. I am saved, the rift restored. In that reunion, I do not fashion my father as better or worse, not into a midget or a monster, but leave him unencumbered, with his dog and his daughter, at peace, unleashed forever in a field of love and forgetting.

❧

CHAPTER 19

The Hardest Gone
the altar of impermanence

IT's USUALLY AT THE BREAK OF DAY, although it can come at any moment.

First up, I take one step into the kitchen and flick the light switch on the wall. A shape stirs by the garden ponds outside the plate glass window, a landscape so still that it can lull you into thinking you see a perfect picture in a frame.

"What is it like to live in a painting?" a guest once enthused about the view from my kitchen sink.

It's not a painting. It's life and, being life, it's equal parts death.

So I recognize the shape that is too fleet to be seen, the finality that is too grim to grasp. It's the heron! One of the reapers that cull our fish on flights north, then south again, two seasons a year.

Up close, herons are exquisitely beautiful. An audience with a heron can freeze you in the shock of good fortune. Only these visitors don't come for a swim, and the good fortune doesn't extend to the fish. Even for a Buddhist, it's difficult to take this sort of outcome sitting down.

The remnants of a heron's hasty visit are ugly. The evidence is criminal. Early on, we fought back. Disbelief gave way to outrage, outrage to combat, and we topped the ponds with nets to foil the enemy. Once.

Trap a bird or any other creature and you'll ensnare yourself in your own cruel ignorance. We never did that again.

But this morning, as the six-foot wingspan unfolds in flight, an orange crescent still gleaming from the beak, I see what's really happening. In an instant, a fish is turned into a bird. Released from one universe and reborn in another. Nothing is lost, but all is transformed.

It takes faith to see, and faith to see far beyond what you can actually see.

This isn't a fish story. It's a matter of life and death. It's all a matter of life and death.

I gave a talk to a group of Buddhists in Philadelphia one time. They listened politely as I told them who knows what. Afterward, a fellow was kind enough to raise his hand. When you speak nonsense to a room of strangers, any response seems rooted in compassion. That's how you know that compassion is our common root.

"I heard you talk about your mother and your teacher, and I was surprised that, as a Buddhist, you referred to them as dead."

No more surprised than I am that they are both, in fact, still dead.

I knew what he was getting at. One of the more intriguing — and promising — things about Buddhism is the concept of reincarnation. Everyone's interested in that.

Let me clip your interest at the quick. I don't know the first thing about reincarnation. I don't know anything about life after death. What I know is that I don't know. And that'll do. Once you stop pretending that you know, you can stop pretending altogether.

What a relief to free myself from decrepit dogma and bullying self-righteousness.

Make no mistake, life and death is the principal concern of all religious inquiry, and no less for me. In Zen, which is rarely given to superlatives, it is called "the great matter." But we don't address the great matter with answers. We address it with questions. We address it the way we address all things. With unwavering attention.

"I know my mother is dead because I buried her," I told the questioner, going on to say that my teacher was cremated, and a part of his femur sits inside a reliquary at the temple where I practice. Their disappearance is not in doubt.

At the same time, I assured the fellow, I've never felt closer to them.

Death is never far away. Life is never far away. Life and death are staring us in the face, in the same way all truth is staring us in the face. Seamless and unceasing motion: appearing, disappearing, never limited by what is seen or unseen. Never ending and so never beginning: eternal and unborn.

A half-swallowed fish, a bird in flight, a leaf turning, a moment arising, my little girl grown, my mother and then me becoming ancestors whose names will surely be lost and forgotten.

Without knowing, without intellectual formulation of any kind, we keep passing beyond a conceptual divide — there to here, then to now, inside to outside, birth to death — across halves that, once penetrated, are revealed as one. This is how it always is, and yet this is how we rarely notice that it is.

Death serves as the notice of life. And when we notice life, really notice, it is the birth of everlasting goodness. We might see through the illusion we've created for ourselves, as separate and inviolable, and do something nice for a change.

Before I got here, a benevolent someone tucked a Jizo statue beside a stand of azaleas in my backyard. A Jizo is a monk with the face of a child. The statue symbolizes kindness and protection, but like all Buddhist imagery, it doesn't represent anything outside of yourself. It reminds us of a quality we each possess that as yet may be unrealized.

Jizo is said to guard the safe passage of travelers in life and death, and particularly women and children. In the way that we are all travelers, and all children, we are each Jizo as well, capable of bringing care and consciousness to every step. Although I don't know who put it here or when, I can say that Jizo left it for Jizo to recognize on sight.

Sometimes when I find out that people need help, that they are struggling with fear or illness, grief, anxiety, or worse, I think, *I'll go into the backyard right now and say a service.* And I just open the door, step into the garden, plant a stick of incense in front of Jizo, and say a chant, which is like a prayer.

Then I come back inside and empty the dishwasher.

Once I started doing that a little, I found myself doing it a lot. I kept hearing about more women, my friends and sisters, strangers and sisters of strangers, waiting for their children, waiting for the news, waiting for arrival, waiting for a turn, waiting for health and optimism, waiting for a safe haven, waiting to start over again.

Although we can't help but keep going, we all need help to keep going.

One day I heard from a woman who with her husband had suffered what some say is the hardest of losses — the loss of a child. They had learned near the end of a pregnancy that the baby they were waiting for wouldn't live after birth. She carried her son until he was born, and then she held him as he died. They were shattered with grief, dazed and displaced, unconsoled by promises, and was there something they could do?

I invited them to the garden, to the Jizo, not to get an answer, but to lay their question to rest. We would remember and ritualize this passage with incense, chanting, and tears. The morning of the service, I found a telltale bird feather a few feet from the Jizo. It was from the heron, and it was no accident.

The couple brought flowers, pinecones, pictures, candy, and tiny treasures to leave behind on our altar of impermanence, which is called the earth. I gave them the feather to take home. It had drifted down like a sad flag on a mast to land in the very place they stood, the place that never leaves, the hereafter.

~

CHAPTER 20

A Better Place

taking the bus back home

I ALWAYS KNEW WHERE IT WOULD LEAD. As we pulled out of the driveway and down the street on the morning drive to nursery school, my daughter piped up from the back seat when the yellow bus rumbled into view.

"My bus, my bus!"

"That's right," I carefully rejoined, "*a bus*," affirming the noun but not yet the pronoun, not the possession, not the slightest quiver of possibility that the public school just down the street would one day be hers. Years before the question of schools could reasonably be raised, I already felt the fluttering clutch of resistance to her baby-talk claim.

Which school for my daughter? I waffled. *Haven't a clue*, I'd think. *Never given it a thought*, I'd shrug, although I'd given plenty of thought to how brilliant her future would be. How bountiful her birthright. How predestined her success. *Perhaps we'll be living in France by then.*

I was not, I thought, unduly anxious about my daughter's prospects. I was not among those employing literacy tutors for three-year-olds. I did not use a spreadsheet to track the process of applying to kindergartens. I did not angle playdates with the grand-children of private-school directors. I did not donate money to the schools at the top of my wish list. I didn't have the money, and I didn't have a list. I simply believed that, one day, when the luminous sheen of my daughter's wonderfulness was made known, something fantastic would happen to transport her to the cusp of greatness.

She was still snapped into a five-point harness in a booster seat. Where, exactly, did I think I was driving her?

To the place we're nearly always driving. Anyplace but here.

Leave it to the children to point so innocently to the problem with this picture.

"Are we there yet?" they keep asking.

Not quite. Almost. A bit farther. A mile higher. And we say, because it sounds so believable, *I'm only doing this for you.*

We applied to the top-ranked private school in the city. They did not take us aside and tell us that our daughter's DNA qualified her for automatic acceptance. We applied as one of four hundred hopefuls paying a $250 fee for a shot at five openings. They did not whisk us to the VIP entrance. We stood, anchored by the weight of our steely ambition, clutching cups of bad coffee with the other no-chance parents one Saturday morning while our children were taken away en masse for their "evaluations." They did not immediately dismiss the others in favor of a clear and unanimous winner. We watched, mortified, as our baby girl bolted from the interview room in hysterics, hollering, "Never bring me here again!"

They did not call us back.

Perhaps she was responding to the critical undercurrent, the menacing pressure we adults were too timid to resist.

Of course, having children has nothing to do with it. We all want something better. Without the better, there is no want. And without want, where would that leave us? This is an answer worth arriving at, providing we don't zoom past it on our way to someplace else.

I'm not opposed to self-determination, to opportunity and mobility. I'm opposed to fear and distrust, to alienation and disaffection. It has poisoned our communities, hollowed our streets and schools and left our sidewalks bare — except for the homeless who make a home where the rest of us might fear to tread. Sometimes I feel lonely on my high patch of green grass. Other times, I might feel cheated and robbed of my sanctuary, threatened, at risk, and on edge.

The problem seems epidemic and the cure, just beyond reach. If you're lucky, you might live in the house or apartment you want, but not the street; the street but not the neighborhood; the neighborhood but not the community; the community but don't get me started on the country! What happened to the country?

On more than one occasion in the past dozen years, my husband and I have bargained with ourselves. If *this* should happen or, heaven forbid, *that*, we would board the first flight into De Gaulle. We belonged in a better place, we told ourselves, but a little something kept getting in the way of our fancy.

One weekend, cooped up with dear old Mom and Dad, our daughter asked a question that reverberates to this day. "Where are my *friends*?" she wailed.

We'd been schlepping sixteen miles round-trip to a progressive preschool, pushing on even farther to the rarely accomplished playdate, and routinely crossing multiple city limits to go to birthday parties. We had an eye on Stanford, our hopes on Harvard, and an in at Cal Tech. We'd gone hunting for her brilliant future, and we'd overlooked her hometown. We'd been chasing her birthright and had ignored her birthplace. *This* was where she lived. This was her world. This was where she wanted to belong. Where *were* her friends? Where are yours?

There are a lot of new communities these days, although almost none of them are the communities where you already live. Disconnected and afraid, we've fashioned other communities that are more like clubs and compounds — virtual or gated, with passwords and private admission. We go there to find people of our like and kind. We call it our tribe. Our circle. Our net. I'm as guilty as you. *Follow my tweets!*

It's a wide world, to be sure, but where's the one you're living in? Where's the one that commands your steady focus and your trusting hand? If you're like we were, it's probably not the one in your backyard. No, we're not there yet.

In the first months after we moved here, my husband and I commenced a minor course of study in gardening. Friends and family sent us books and manuals; we sought expert advice. We considered ourselves daft and dangerous: a threat to an undefended paradise.

I read a short history of horticulture before I dared turn a spade of dirt. That's how I learned that the word *paradise* originated in Persia, where it meant a walled outdoor area, natural or planted, for sport or pleasure. Only later did the word take on its fantastical meaning. A true paradise is as real as your own backyard, and never anywhere else. Let the etymologists quibble over the difference: I've seen it with my own eyes.

The view that there is higher ground apart from the place we occupy is based entirely on ignorance. It perpetuates fear and, worse, enlarges it. There is only one place. The one you're in. You can never leave, but you can turn it inside out. Do you want to live in friendship or fear? Paradise or paranoia? We are each citizens of the place we make, so make it a better place.

At the grocery store, give your place in line to the person behind you.

Ask the checker how her day is going, and mean it.

On the way out, give your pocket money to the solicitor at the card table no matter what the cause.

Buy a cup of lemonade from the kids at the sidewalk stand. Tell them to keep the change.

Roll down your car window when you see the homeless man on the corner with the sign. Give him money. Have no concern over what he will do with it.

Smile at him. It will be the first smile he has seen in a very long time.

Do not curse your neighbor's tall grass, weeds, foul temperament, or house color. Given time, things change by themselves. Even your annoyance.

Thank the garbageman. Be patient with the postal worker.

Leave the empty parking space for someone else to take. They will feel lucky.

Buy cookies from the Girl Scout and a sack of oranges from the poor woman standing in the broiling heat at the intersection.

Talk to strangers about the weather.

Allow others to be themselves, with their own point of view. If you judge them, you are in error.

Do not let difference make a difference.

Do not despair over the futility of your impact or question the outcome.

Do not pass while the lights are flashing.

Trusting life means trusting where you are, and trusting where you'll go, and trusting the way in between, as on a bus trip, the driving left to someone else. It's bumpy but remarkably reliable.

Our daughter goes to the public school down the street. The hallways are a little scruffy. The classrooms are crowded. The kids are just neighborhood kids. She calls them her friends, and she has far more friends than I do. The money there is scarce, but the opportunity is wide open and free. You might think it is a brave thing to do, but we can be brave. We were born in the home of the brave.

On the first day of kindergarten, the teacher stood before an array of beautiful faces. She spoke loudly to reach the pack of teary parents spectating at the back of the room.

"Our job is to create citizens," she declared, and turned to face the flag. I placed my hand over my heart with allegiance.

The school has nothing to do with it. Choose whatever school you like. It's all about the bus. I'm on it, and there's a seat beside me with your name on it.

CHAPTER 21

Making Peace

knowing when to quit

g RANDMA HAD A DEEP BASIN at the back of her kitchen, by the screen door, and beside it a tub washer with a wringer on top.

On wash days, which were whole days, she wrangled a mound of laundry from one pile to the next. Greasy work shirts, overalls, and dungarees; handkerchiefs; rags, aprons, and towels, rubbed raw. White sheets and pillowcases. The straight cotton shift she called her housedress. (She had a few, and they were identical, save the flowered fabric, sewn from a single pattern and worn for a week before washing.) The dainty half-slips that peeked beneath her hem, long johns, brassieres, and underdrawers, the glimpse of which could pinken my cheeks.

Once each load had rumbled around the tub, we hauled it out wet and sloshed it in the basin until the wringing began.

I didn't have to be warned to keep my fingers away from the crush of the twin rollers, but Grandma let me stand clear and pull the flattened half from the other side and fold it like a stretch of taffy into the basket below.

She had a clothesline out back in the grass. I was too small to reach it, but I could hold the bottom end of things as she wedged the pins in place. The line filled up over the morning and past noon, when the stiff shapes softened and fluttered like prayer flags in the dry breeze beneath the spires of the cedar trees.

I tell you this so I can hear it myself. I tell it so I can know her quiet pain and her secret suffering, and so I can know yours too.

Things aren't quite what they seem.

It might have started on a wash day, or the next day, but soon it would be every day that Grandma did what none of us would ever see her do: reach for a tumbler and pour the port wine that kept her company in the hours after our leaving. After her son, my father, had left for good, her grandchildren scattered, her table emptied, and her body withered, the days were foreshortened by dark cynicism and embittering disease. She started one day and she never quit.

We didn't know. My parents got the call from my grandfather when she was too far gone to forbid him otherwise, and after the paramedics had lifted her out of the bed from which she could no longer rise. I didn't hear much about what happened next. I heard only what she said in the hospital, at the very end, when my mother and father came to stand at her side.

She said, "Look who's here."

Life is suffering. No one can make less of it. Pain finds us without fail. Hearts break; dreams die; hatred flourishes; sickness prevails; people and promises leave without a trace. I dare not trivialize. I only dare to turn toward the glimmer and let it lift me into a moment's radiant grace. This is the turn we have to take, over and over, to make our way home, to reach the untrammeled peace, the pure marvel, of an ordinary life. We must finally see that the light we seek streams from our very own eyes and always has.

When my two sisters and I were really little, my mother drove us to our babysitter's house early each morning so she could go to work as a teacher. Two of us walked to school from there, and my little sister stayed at the sitter's all day.

We sat in the back as my mom drove the familiar few miles of the daily route. This was before car seats, it was even before seatbelts, so you won't be shocked to hear that my little sister stood on the hump of the floorboard and gripped the back of the front seat as we rode. She would stand up and speak into my mom's right ear.

Turn here! Turn here!

My baby sister wasn't giving my mom directions to the sitter's house; she was giving her directions *away* from the sitter's house. It was so funny: as if just hearing the words would cause my mom to steer away from an everyday destination, a place she could find in her sleep.

My mom, of course, couldn't turn. But I can, and I do, every time I wake up.

All practice is the practice of making a turn in a different direction. Toward one thing and away from another: the particulars in any situation don't matter, because we always know the right way. A different way. With practice, you get better at turning.

Turn here! Turn here!

This is my practice. It is not anything special you need to learn. It is not some new information you need to get. It is nothing you haven't heard before. It is just a turn you might not yet have made, or made again, and again, and again. A turn toward intimate engagement with the life you already have.

The instructions are in your hands. And when you follow them, you arrive clear and fresh — free of heartache, failure, fear, anger, and judgment — into a ready-made life of deep peace and genuine satisfaction. Fulfillment derives not from lofty achievements, but from ordinary feats. It arrives not once in a lifetime, but every moment of the livelong day.

To find it, look in the laundry, the kitchen, and the yard.

I'm told that readers like to be taken on a journey. I'm sure that's true, but this adage frustrates and perplexes me. The fact is, you're already on a journey — a sometimes desperate, painful, and disappointing journey. You take this journey every day and night, and, even given the information and encouragement to quit going one way and toward another, you might not. It's hard, I know, but it's the only way home.

The journey ends with one awakening turn. Here.

And so I've said all this, too much, and no better than my grandmother in her unwitting epitaph. *Look who's here.*

I know when to quit looking someplace else, and now you do too.

Sort the light from the dark, the delicate from the indestructible, and the heavy duty from the hand wash cold. Empty the basket, and empty it again. That's the wonderful thing about laundry: it never ends.

To study the Way is to study oneself.
To study oneself is to forget oneself.
To forget oneself is to be enlightened
by the ten thousand things.
And this traceless enlightenment continues forever.

— DOGEN ZENJI, 1233

epilogue

～

Airing Dirty Laundry

Y OU'VE JUST FINISHED A BOOK titled *Hand Wash Cold,* and with good reason you might still wonder exactly how to do what the title says. Let me oblige your interest.

1. Wipe the dried toothpaste from a sink or rinse the motor oil from a pail.
2. Fill your receptacle with cold water.
3. Add a drizzle of expensive laundry detergent or a spritz of dishwashing liquid to the water.
4. Slosh the liquid around to conjure up a few bubbles.
5. Submerge garment in water.

6. Let it sit.

7. Hours or even days later, remember.

8. Rinse in clear, cold water. This delicate item is probably not the kind of thing that can survive a decent squeeze.

9. Which means that, when you take it out, you'll have to hang it up over the bathtub to let the water drip out of it.

10. And that will probably cause the fabric dye to drip out of it too, creating streaks of variable intensity and lasting regret.

11. When it dries, your favorite article of clothing will be six inches longer than when you purchased it. Or six inches shorter. Or six inches longer on one side, six inches shorter on the other.

12. You might wish that you had laid it flat to dry, which would take so long that it would mildew before you could wear it again.

All this effort will allow you to wear the garment once before you resolve to (a) never buy anything else that has to be hand washed cold, or (b) never wash it, thereby transcending all questions and eliminating all doubt.

You can learn how to meditate by visiting any practice center near you, or by joining me at my practice home, the Hazy Moon Zen

Center in Los Angeles (www.hazymoon.com). There, you'll find classes and retreats especially for beginners, along with invigorating and inspiring talks. You might also find, like the spare change that turns up in the bottom of the washer, a modest fortune of another kind: an old teacher. I encourage you to see for yourself.

acknowledgments

*t*here comes a time to thank the people who never need to be thanked:

My parents and grandparents, who loved as best they could and more than I'll ever know.

My sisters, Patricia Heinrich and Susan Tate, who grant me my place and always meet me in the middle.

My forever friend, Robin Cavanaugh, the scout on a rescue mission.

My agent, Ted Weinstein, whose patience surpasses all standards of faith.

My editor, Georgia Hughes, who shares my daughter's name,

who shares my grandfather's name: all told, three farmers who never fail to see the real me.

My teacher, Nyogen Yeo Roshi, who mirrors my devotion to the Dharma and shares my undying love for the master gardener Maezumi Roshi.

Lastly, my husband, Ed Miller, who gives me the means and the motivation to start another load each day, and to love it.

No one could ask for more.

index of lost socks

ᵔ

every load seems to leave a little something missing. You can retrace your steps all day long and still not find what was left behind. Use this shortcut to locate life's irreplaceables when they have disappeared from sight.

WHEN YOU'RE LOOKING FOR:	SEE CHAPTER:
Acceptance	5, 8, 10, 17, or 20
Adventure	1, 7, 9, or 15
Attention	5, 7, 10, 13, or 16
Authenticity	1, 5, 7, 12, or 14

index of lost socks